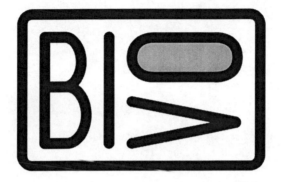

A Modern-Day Guide for Bi-Vocational Saints

Leveraging All of Life into One Calling

HUGH HALTER

BiVo: A Modern-Day Guide for Bi-Vocational Saints.
Copyright © 2013 by Hugh Halter
Published by Missio Publishing in Littleton, CO. Visit us at
missiopublishing.com. All rights reserved.

print ISBN: 978-0-983086-4-44
ebook ISBN: 978-0-9899578-1-6

Published in association with Samizdat Creative, a division of
Samizdat Publishing Group (samizdatcreative.com).

Cover design: Jarrod Joplin (jarrodjoplin.com)

Table of Action

(contents don't do much for you)

The Ship Has Tipped

We had just spent two days in a whirlwind tour of Disney World with our family. It was a great time, but being an introvert who doesn't really enjoy millions of sweaty Disney zombies, 100-degree heat, 98% humidity or hot dogs that cost fourteen dollars, I couldn't wait to park the minivan and enjoy one last night on the Fort Meyers beach. I unloaded the bags and told Cheryl, "I'm outta here. I'm going to take a good long run along the beach. I need some caveman time to myself."

After a three-mile jog along serene turquoise water, I turned around and made it another mile before pooping out. I slowed to a walk and enjoyed a well-needed conversation with God about a lot of things that had been on my mind about my calling, our church, and a few hundred other complaints and concerns. Somewhere between deep thoughts and watching pelicans dive for fish, I noticed a sunburned father kissing his kids and wife goodbye as he prepared to take off on a rather large catamaran.

It was really windy and I found myself wondering how this apparent novice was going to navigate this rather large vessel by himself. Through the howling wind, the instructor was yelling out directives but the man seemed uninterested and just wanted to set sail. He jumped on, grabbed the rope to the main sail, and the rental operator shoved him off the shore. No more than five feet out on his maiden voyage, a huge 40-50 mph gust filled the sails and the boat shot off the shore like a cat out of a bathtub. The wife put her hands on top of her head, the instructor's eyes got as big as saucers, and I noticed a few other people now attuned to the unfolding drama.

The man on the rocket-launched schooner? Oh, he was lying face down on the deck trying to hold on and keep the sail in the right spot. Did he know the right spot? I wasn't sure. As the vessel reached about 400 yards off the shore, a collective scream shot out from the beach as we all watched the catamaran tip up on one side and then suddenly flip over, sending

Captain Cook flying into the sea. We were all relieved to see him swimming back to the overturned boat, but we all knew that his next stop would be Cuba unless he got some help from the shore. I looked at several men around me and without saying a word, we all dove in and swam toward the disaster zone.

After an exhausting swim out, I made it to the vessel first. The man was quite happy to see me and couldn't stop saying thank you. Trying to calm him, I said, "So it looks like you got caught with your pants down a bit, ay?"

He sort of laughed but remained pretty sober.

"I'd say you're pretty courageous to try this in what people say is the hammerhead capital of the U.S.!" I added.

He just stared at me as if to say, *That is the dumbest thing to say in a time like this.*

"So do you know how to pull this thing back over?" I asked.

Yelling through the whistling wind, he said, "Not at all. I actually never planned for this to happen. I'm clueless!"

Fortunately, the other men arrived, and one of them knew how to right the ship and we all got it back to shore. Barely!

This story serves as a simple metaphor for what I believe is happening inside the church.

The downwardly mobile world

You may have noticed the world of ministry has changed because the world has changed. No need for statistics and long, drawn out ammo to persuade you. If you've been a concerned Christian or professional saint, you know things are shifting. Economically, the world is in turmoil and no one can balance a budget. Upward mobility is becoming a thing of the past, and those under the age of forty will most likely be the first generation to fail at out-earning their parents. The economics of the world are deeply affecting the economics of the church in more ways that just money. Because of the desperate focus on having or maintaining jobs, people move on average almost every five years to keep pace. In Denver alone, the average metro or suburban citizen moves every eighteen months, and thus churches have to operate based on the probability of losing many of their congregational members every few years, just like a college ministry. Ministry therefore may not be able to be based on sustainability, but rather on pure blind faithfulness to make disciples one by one.

As people lose their sense of stability, security and sustainability, their tendency is to move from generosity to scarcity—they simply won't give like they used to. At present, the average Christian gives to the church at the exact percentage non-believers give to charities—just fewer than three percent. Culturally, those under forty have shifted in their value sets. Fifty years ago, one of the highest virtues was "loyalty," and people would give faithfully to the church, trusting the institution and the leaders to use the money wisely. And even if they didn't agree with a building fund or focus for the corporate finances, they would continue to give simply because they trusted the spiritual hierarchy. Not anymore.

Today's believers are not loyal or blindly trusting. One of their highest values is "meaning," and they will only give to what they see is making a visible difference, or what they perceive will bring them meaning at a personal level. You may argue with this at a philosophical level, but you will not be able to fight it at the street level. People, even those inside the church, are exhausted at giving to boxes or buildings whose influence is waning, and they simply won't give to keep the lights on or pay the staff. They want to help real people with real needs.

These rough seas, brought about by the winds of global change, are going to keep blowing, and the collective unconscious and conscious atmosphere, values, and ethos for practical living and kingdom building have been forever changed. Black and white is now grey. Generosity, faithfulness, kingdom impact, and God's design for building His church are now vast question marks with unlimited opportunities. Those that navigate well will not only survive but thrive in this new world.

The downwardly mobile church

In 2013, the Carnival cruise ship *The Triumph* lost power off the coast of the Yucatan peninsula. The voyage for consumers who had hoped for a beautiful, restful and enjoyable cruise turned into a nightmare as they had to be towed over a week's time back to Alabama. The toilets stopped, the air-conditioning failed, the food spoiled, and the travelers realized that their dream vacation was not worth a penny, let alone the thousands they had spent.

This is a picture of the failing consumer church—large, medium and micro forms. Yes, there will always be churches that seem to be avoiding all these shifts—churches that show growth based on old measurements and who seem to be growing both numerically and financially—but don't be fooled by these aberrations. Wise leaders look beyond the occasional success story and instead stare honestly at the undeniable trends. In seasons of economic struggle, what always occurs is a growing chasm between the haves and the have nots. As church attendance declines nationally, and as we fail on a global scale to see new disciples made, mega churches and growing churches are tasting what could be the last wave of transfer growth before the reality of the trends hit home. Regardless of the size of the ship you serve in, calculating leaders must adjust to the trends.

The western church's business model based on the expectation of growth, optimism, and promise of financial blessing has proven to be a consumer nightmare. We've tried to attract people with safety for our kids, hand sanitizers in every hallway, programs, preaching, and worship that look more like a carnival theatre night, and what have we gotten for all our spiritual protection and provision? A harbor full of drifting ships who have lost power and are quickly losing the return customers we thought would always stay with us. Many churches are leveraged to the max, and the engines are decelerating at best or have totally shut down at worst. Like the tugboats that slowly pull the massive vessels back to port, God has not abandoned ship, but is pulling us back for a serious retrofit. We need a new model of disciple making, a new model of doing church, a new vision for our lives and what our money and time can accomplish.

By the year 2025, America will be as unchurched as the rest of the western world. As a consultant to church plants, mega-churches, traditional churches, denominations, para-church and missions agencies, the most conservative advice I can give is to tell you that the old is now passing away. Gone are the days when a young man or woman can graduate from Bible school or seminary and find a great church to go work for. Like the man caught on the catamaran, people are being hurled into the unknown without any vision or practical skills for how to follow God and lead people.

Will the real church please stand up?

But despite all this negativity, there is a silver lining. The church, at least the real one that God is building, is not just the buildings, the structures, programs or paradigms of ministry. The church is the people of God, and what that means is that all of us, both paid and unpaid, are feeling the pain together.

The questions for some are how do we keep our churches alive, sustainable, vibrant, and open to God's voice?

The questions for others are how am I to live, how can I live a life after God that my children will want to follow and emulate, how do I play a role in

God's kingdom when I can't stand going to church? I could go on with many more honest questions, but suffice it to say that everyone, at least those who truly care about Jesus and his kingdom movement, should care about The Church.

During my sabbatical in 2013, my nineteen-year-old daughter asked me what I was thinking about doing after twenty-five years of pastoring. I'll admit, I was pooped out and would have loved to call for a sub or just tap out for a while, and she sensed it. "So, Dad, you're not thinking of leaving our church are you?"

"Well, babe, everything is on the table. So, maybe." I responded. To my surprise, she said angrily, "Dad, you have to keep pastoring and leading us. I've now seen other churches and I'm around other Christians all the time who hate their churches and are barely making it spiritually."

Then she asked, "Do you know how different we are, how unique our people and our story is? Dad, any of my friends, both Christian and especially the ones that aren't, would love Adullam. In fact, we need our type of church to take over the world."

With that one ten minute conversation, I was hooked again. But what does it mean for me, and maybe you, to work with God in building His church in a world that seems so unattracted to our churchy ways? If God were to shine bright through his people, his church, what would it cost me, or us?

Yes, there will always be churches that expand through transfer growth and that can keep their pastors paid and their churchy folks happy and safe, but what about the rest of us who are no longer content to simply exist in the religious zone? What about those of us who can't play the games anymore, who don't want to keep consumer Christians happy? What will it truly cost if we take Jesus' words seriously, and I mean all of his words? Is it possible that Jesus has a plan for us?

I would not only answer with a whole-hearted *Yes!* but I would also say that Jesus is glad we are finally feeling enough pain to look up, ask hard questions, and turn to him for his answers. I believe that currents of change are helping us drift back toward His design for our lives and the church. And true change always begins with some struggle before harmony settles in. God's mission is not dependent upon the things we think it is. It never has been. And once we acknowledge this and recalibrate, I believe we will find a creative new story that not only feels better at a life level, but also makes sense to people who are trying to find God and the good news of kingdom life.

Jesus is trying to set us free, which also means

he is trying to free the church, but we must let him challenge us at the level of the wallet.

As Jesus plainly said, "You cannot serve both God and money," and thus every aspect of our faith, fears, plans, and dreams will be challenged at this basic level. Currency is the control switch of both building his kingdom and building our own kingdoms, and the leaders of God's evolving church will be those who can lean into the tension and find a pure path through it all. If we don't tack to ways of his kingdom, if we don't open our sails to the wind of the Holy Spirit, we will soon find ourselves dwindling under the hot sun in a quiet, drifting, fruitless void. It's time to accept the change and let Jesus teach us anew how to lighten the loads of these other kingdoms and let him leverage us to the hilt.

Who will survive?

Those who have courage to think, look, and function outside the box. Those who cast off pure dependence on others, blind dependence upon a church, or expect God to make ministry easy. Jesus has always led his missional saints into the tension of kingdom life and kingdom provision. The gospel came to us through a church of barely paid and non-paid saints, and we can once again recover the beautiful freedom that will bring the gospel to the next epoch of history.

The bank, or our model of church isn't the only thing broke

But this isn't just about the church or your ministry calling. This book is really about you. Beyond the dollars and cents of ministry are hundreds of thousands of faithful saints who really do want to serve the world, but who now struggle to stay afloat. Treading water isn't just about financial survival. It's also about spiritual survival. As I've talked to waves of leaders both young and old, the pain of the church has gotten them close to shipwrecking their souls. "How could God let this happen to me? How do I manage my true faith amidst the lies I've seen in the organized church? How do I live faithfully after Christ without pandering to the consumer whims of the next cruise ship to go down?" These and a hundred other deep questions cause the present and future leaders of the church to question their very calling. We were sold a bill of goods that told us if we could preach well, organize staff, and run weekend programs, we would be honored, respected, followed, and provided for. But none of that is true. The skills that once gave us meaning have left us yearning for more. But where do we go to learn the new skills and the new way of life for God's legitimate leaders?

I may fail to deliver, but it is my heart to try

to provide at least a start for you to rethink your vision, renew your faith, restore your heart, and re-imagine a fruitful and even fun life of service to the King of Glory.

Ministry Angle ▷ **Leveraged Kingdom Life** ◁ Secular Angle

This book is for present church leaders, but it is mostly written for the future leaders of God's movement. We use the term *BiVo* to simply mean those who learn to blend two primary callings. The first is to work to provide for ourselves and our family.

As the scriptures say in 2 Thessalonians 3:6-10,

> In the name of the Lord Jesus Christ, we command you, brothers and sisters, to keep away from every believer who is idle and disruptive and does not live according to the teaching you received from us. For you yourselves know how you ought to follow our example. We were not idle when we were with you, nor did we eat anyone's food without paying for it. On the contrary, we worked night and day, laboring and toiling so that we would not be a burden to any of you. We did this, not because we do

> not have the right to such help, but in
> order to offer ourselves as a model for
> you to imitate. For even when we were
> with you, we gave you this rule: "The
> one who is unwilling to work shall not
> eat.

The second is to see our entire lives leveraged and in use for God's kingdom purposes, to live intentionally as a missionary saint. As Paul said in Galatians 2:20,

> I have been crucified with Christ and I
> no longer live, but Christ lives in me.
> The life I now live in the body, I live by
> faith in the Son of God, who loved me
> and gave himself for me.

I believe every believer is called to these two callings or vocations or jobs, if you will, and so a business owner, employee climbing the corporate ladder, stay at home mother, as well as anyone in a vocational ministry position share these callings. The issue is whether you are moving toward a life that pleases Jesus and is leveraged for his purposes. Some of you reading will be coming from the angle of a "ministry position" where a percentage of your income comes from work in a church, para-church, missions agency, etc. Others of you are coming from the angle of a secular vocation—whether you are a lawyer, stay at home mom, school teacher, or own your own business, you are also trying to figure out how to leverage your capacity for Christ.

This book is designed to pull everyone in for a huddle to discuss something we should all care about. And that is whether or not God's church (all of us working together) will reflect the glory for which it was intended as we make God's kingdom tangible. The church must be viewed as the people of God, not the institution. So the fate of the church is really the fate of each Christ follower. The issue of stewarding our families, our finances, and our collective mission to make God's kingdom tangible to the world excludes no one, and I hope that this short book will spark a vision for your life, your leadership, and a movement of true good news to the world.

If you want to keep believing that you'll have a job, that you can spend forty hours a week working on a sermon for a smiling congregation that trusts you and wants to hang on every word you utter from the raised platform, this is not the read for you. This book is for the rest of you. The ones who no longer want to prop up the present paradigm of church that is drifting upside down in the white-caps. It's for the rest of us who have been laid off, let go, or left to manage on our own. This book is for the courageous ones who, out of a sense of adventure, had hopped onto the "full-time ministry" catamaran and enjoyed the brief exhilaration of jetting out into the turquoise seas, but who now realize trouble is waiting for anyone who won't look up and find a new way to sail. This book is also for business leaders who want every penny they make, every person they hire and work with, every invest-ment they make, to count in the heavenlies.

Key ideas about this story, this book, and your life

- The gospel means "good news" and is always available regardless of world trends, economic downturns, or seasonal struggles.
- The good news of God's kingdom comes with cheap DNA, cheap environments, and leaders who are abundantly available without exces-sive costs. Thus movement is cheap, too.
- The church is the "people of God" so if the people of God live good news, the church will be good news, regardless of how the weekend programs and presentations are.
- Much of our ministry misery is self-imposed because we have bought into the consumer

trap that sucks the life of God out of our actual life. Financial freedom brings ministry freedom!

- Making disciples is easier and cheaper than keeping consumer Christians happy.
- Everyone's calling is of equal importance, although we each live out our callings differently.
- Personal meaning can never be found in a role, business card, title, or salary. Meaning comes from personal clarity and obedience to what God calls us to do.
- Full-time vocational ministry (American-style) is not normal (less than 200 years old) and there are exciting opportunities for ministry in bi-vocational or volunteer paradigms.
- If none of us got paid, God would still expect us to lead and serve the world.

The goal of our calling isn't to be bi-vocational, fully paid, or volunteer. The goal of our existence is to learn how to leverage everything God has given us.

Nimbility

Okay, enough with the bad news. This book is mostly about what I think is great news—that is, with a little inertia you can live a wildly influential life while still meeting the mundane challenges in front of you. I don't view all the difficult changes in the world as bad. I think they push us to passionately architect our lives so that we are as free to live for God, really live! To be flexible, able to stop or turn on a dime. To be quick to adjust, unconstrained by the chains that hold most people down. This is what I mean by nimbility. The gospel is wide open to you, and if you are open to a little re-org of your life, you can experience greater freedom at both a personal and financial level. My personal story is the basis for this book and my hope is that you will take it seriously for your own life. Not just your ministry, but *for your life.*

In my mind and heart, I've been in full time ministry since I felt God "call me" as a junior in high school. After I graduated, I went to a university and got a double major in psychology and religion before heading right into seminary, fully expecting to become a paid professional pastor of some type. After two years of seminary, I met my wife Cheryl, adopted her five-year-old son who had a doozy of an epilepsy condition, and at the age of twenty-four had to postpone seminary in order to work to provide for my family. I restarted a house painting business that paid my way through college, and for the first five years of our marriage I worked thirty to forty hours a week with the brush and then another thirty hours a week for Youth for Christ. I did try to raise a little missionary support, but it was nothing I could count on, so painting paid the bills.

After another five-year grind (all the while thinking I would get back to seminary) my wife and I decided to start a church for all the people we had seen come to faith. We had added two more girls to our family, so the pressure and privilege of providing for my growing family while we started a church community was a daily juggle. Each week was literally a brush-stroke and prayer. I would paint whenever I got work, and if nothing came up I would jam my days full of people. When I did have to paint, I would adjust and meet groups of men in the morning before work, at lunch, and then after work on the way home. Ryan's disability didn't let us get much sleep, so after a quick nap in parking lots before I headed home, I'd lock into family time and then Cheryl and I would open our home and get through weekend church duties. It wasn't easy, and many weeks would have qualified in the "brutal" category. But God was faithful and both my family and church grew. After five years, I was making about $2500 a month through the church so it took the pressure off of full time painting, but I was clearly living what we would now call a bi-vocational life.

After we resigned from the first church plant, we went on staff with a missions consulting agency and again I put my hand to raising support. It went a little better this time, accounting for about half of our monthly needs. But with an expensive brain surgery for Ryan and normal living expenses, the house painting got us through the next five years again.

Many of you got to know our story at this next transition. We moved to Denver and, while maintaining some missionary support, began a small missionary team to model—what many know as The Tangible Kingdom. We eventually wrote our story in a book by the same title, but essentially it was our second church plant. I again had to go back to house painting, but this time as the church grew we intentionally decided to try an experiment. We wanted to see if God could truly build his church without all the money pressure. As we formed our bi-laws, we locked into a "bi-vocational" orientation that would prove to be the most important foundation stones we would lay.

As with any church plant, it was a struggle, but it worked. And as our story was told, people were inspired by how we engaged the culture, formed gospel communities of mission, and then emerged as a viable congregational network. Over the last five years, I've shared our story with many thousands of Christian leaders and normal folks, and the single most intriguing aspect of our story that people want us to talk about is the bi-vocational element. We're now on year nine of our church in Denver and I still only receive one third of my monthly income from it. In a few chapters, I'll pull the sheets off of our story so you can see everything exposed, but suffice it to say that while we continue to mentally and emotionally feel called to full time ministry, I have to work thirty to forty hours a week outside the church to make it happen. After twenty-five years, I now feel that God hemmed me into this life because he knew that some other people, maybe thousands, needed to see some alternatives.

A disclaimer is probably needed at this point. My intention for sharing this story isn't to deconstruct everything about ministry and church and money. I believe that making a full time living from the gospel is biblical and if you can do it, I am very happy for you. As with any transition in church history, it doesn't change all at once and so I hope that many will continue to enjoy the freedom that comes from a full time salary. But transitions also mean that many thousands, maybe even millions, of people will be caught in the carnage of change. And so my heart is to reconstruct some alternative pictures of kingdom reality for those of you who need to see hope for life and ministry outside the boxes of full-time church work.

The gospel costs—just not that much money!

Early on in our church plant experience in Denver, my buddy Matt and I were sitting at a local Starbucks. We had just experienced some really tough stuff with another team member, the people we were reaching had massive life issues that weren't working out very well, and both Matt and I were frustrated at how tight we were financially. As we talked it over, I said, "The Gospel just costs." Matt, however, noticed that although there is incredible cost personally and with our time and delaying or completely deferring our own goals of easy living, our costs were still quite small compared to what the gospel cost Jesus and millions of followers who have literally given everything for Jesus.

I don't want to make it seem like it's easier to live bi-vocationally or change your entire paradigm of ministry and life. For sure, there are great difficulties with changing the paradigm of church, money, family, calling, discipleship, and faithfulness, and we will be honest with you about all the pitfalls, but I hope you'll see that the beauty far outweighs the struggle.

Here at the beginning, I want to make sure you know that my intention is not to belittle or challenge those who help lead God's church in a full time, paid capacity. As well, I don't want to make it sound as if the only biblical way to proceed forward is to be bi-vocational. Bi-vocational is not the goal, but it can and will be an emerging option to get to the goal. The goal is to make God famous throughout the world and it's a vision big enough to include anyone, those who are fully paid, those who are partially paid, and most importantly, those who will never get paid. Regardless, every person needs to learn how to let God leverage three primary spheres of life.

The three primary leverage points

So, how we make a living or how much our living makes isn't the goal. The goal or aim of our lives is to let God leverage what he has given us. In other words, each one of us, according to the parable of the talents, is given a certain hand to play, and whether you are dealt pocket aces or the dreaded 2,9 unsuited combo, we can learn to leverage what we have for God's glory. As we go through this book, I want you to keep these three primary leverage points in view. If you maximize all three of them, you will live the best life possible.

They are business for mission, family on mission, and counter-culture mission.

Business for mission

God has given men and women the capacity and calling to make a living. Whether it is living off the land or living off the nine-to-five, the job itself and the ability to work is God given. Most people I know complain about their work, always try to get out of it, or view it as a hindrance to God's mission. I can count on one hand the friends I've had who wake up in the morning to fulfill their mission through work. But Jesus worked and we are called to follow him. Thus we must view all our business enterprise as kingdom building. Every second on the job and every penny earned is a resource or leverage that God can use if we change our thinking on the issue. 1 Thessalonians 4:11-12 says,

> Make it your goal to live a quiet life, minding your own business and working with your hands, just as we instructed you before. Then people who are not Christians will respect the way you live, and you will not need to depend on others. (NLT)

Your secular work is the soil in which God plants his sacred kingdom work. Therefore your work is not a hindrance to what God is doing, but instead a significant part of what he is doing.

Family on mission

God builds his church on people and, as he began with Peter, he keeps building this divine community on human beings, not buildings or programs. Thus, a church will never be missional unless people learn to be a missional family. This includes our friends we go on mission with and, most of all, it includes our literal families. The family, the father and mother, brother and sister, and extended and blended family was the primary means by which the gospel message was passed down and the gospel life was lived out. Just like many view their jobs as a hindrance to enjoying life or serving God, many people view their family as a hindrance, or at least a huge distraction. Others would love to see their family on mission, but believe that the present brokenness of the marriage or parent to child relationship is so bad that they just can't. Many who are in the early child-rearing years throw up their hands in exhaustion and pull out of mission because they simply haven't been coached through how to recognize the missional possibilities in every season of life. But just like God will leverage our jobs, God also loves to leverage our family for his purposes. People consider the reality of God when they see normal people living for God, and there is no greater opportunity to evoke curiosity or find common ground from which to inspire people than how you do marriage, family, and close friends.

Counter-culture mission

"No one else dared join them, even though they were highly regarded by the people." This one sentence of Acts 5:13 gives us a picture of how unique the burgeoning Christian community was and how people viewed them from the outside. The new people of God were clearly a counter-cultural community. It didn't happen overnight, and it remains a constant struggle, but God's missionary saints were known as people who were counter to the culture of debt, of social exclusion, of idolatry, of overwork, and of legalistic requirements. As they learned kingdom ways of living, they went against the culture of religion and they went against the culture of family, tradition, and custom.

Leverage is about the influence of people who truly Sabbath, who are financially free of debt, who are free of paralyzing family expectations, and who are free of concern for what any human being thinks of them. They stand out like salt among decaying meat. They look like a bright light amidst darkness. They look like they are from another kingdom. They are good news! The gospel is not about trying to wedge a little Jesus into our crazy lives. The gospel is about letting God bring redemption and the way of his crazy kingdom into our frantically dysfunctional patterns of living. Being a disciple is moving from unbelief to belief in every part of your life. As we do that we will go against every cultural norm, which is not something to fear. It is good news!

As you go through this book, we will help you develop these three leverage points and provide resources or point you to resources to help you gain this God-given advantage. The Lord wants you to influence the world and has given you everything you need to do it in life and godliness. But you cannot live the same and find these pearls of great price. You have to do a gut check.

Questions that might change your life

1. If money were neither a hindrance nor a focus, what would you want to wake up every morning and do? In other words, what would be good news to you?

2. If the world keeps moving the way it is and church decline continues in the West, how much pain do you need to feel before you will consider alternative forms of funding for your livelihood and mission?

3. Would you be willing to make less from ministry funding if you could find some friends and band together to create a viable mission and simple church expressions and experiences? Would this be a preferable life?

Kiss of Death

You cannot serve both God and money

In John 12, we have story that is our story. It is within a week of Jesus' impending death. The Passover is in view and Jesus is reclining in the home of Simon the leper. Lazarus, Martha, as well as the disciples are there. A woman named Mary stoops down and pours a large amount of perfumed oil on Jesus' feet. This beautiful moment between Jesus and his closest friends is interrupted with harsh words from Judas who belittles Mary by suggesting that the money wasted on Jesus could have been used more appropriately to serve the poor. According to the scriptures, Judas could really care less about the poor, and was truly upset because he was in charge of their collective purse. And as the treasurer to the disciples and Jesus, he had developed a secret vice of occasionally skimming a little money off the top.

It was after this dinner that Judas went and asked the governing authorities how much he could get for handing Jesus over to them. They agreed on thirty shekels (roughly four months' wages). The die was cast, and Judas, a young man who had walked beside Jesus for three years, who had seen the beauty of his life, who no doubt had countless personal moments walking, laughing with, and having Jesus minister to him personally, was now about to sell out his friend for a paycheck. He was about to give the kiss of death. Judas goes down in history as one of the worst individuals ever. How could he do that to such a perfect man? How could he be so shortsighted? How could his life and words be so full of hypocrisy?

These questions for Judas are the same questions we must answer.

We, like Judas, have experienced the beauty of Jesus. We have benefited from him. He has changed our lives and our minds about what is most important in life, and yet we, just like Judas, struggle to keep a sense of purity between the true essence of kingdom life and ministry and our concern for personal security.

Was Judas a bad guy? Probably not. Just like us. Judas loved Jesus. But like two horses pulling the chariot of the king, one horse runs pure, looking straight ahead and faithfully pulling, while the other horse looks around, gets distracted and allows concerns and anxieties to cloud his vision. When the two horses fought inside Judas, eventually a choice was made to use Jesus for his own ends.

Judas had a conflict between manna and mammon.

Manna or mammon: Gut check time

As a metaphor for coming out of stifling spiritual bondage, Moses was leading God's people through their self-created wilderness. Not only to provide food, but also to retrain them to trust in him alone, God sends manna from heaven. He provided enough for the entire nation each day, but nothing more. Every night, with full bellies, every father would tuck his children in and then lie awake wondering if there would be enough for them the next day.

As most of us would, many people woke up early to try to hit the fields first and store up extra, just in case God stopped providing. But manna isn't about extra. Manna is about daily provision for today. Just today. Manna was God's way of teaching us all that he is faithful to provide, and he always will be.

By the time we get to the Judas story, another word for provision is used. In Matthew 6:24, which most scholars believe was Jesus' primary teaching on how his new kingdom would work, he lays out the scaffolding that his church would be built on, or more personally, the framework that our lives would be built on, saying,

> No one can serve two masters. Either you will hate the one and love the other, or you will be devoted to the one and despise the other. You cannot serve both God and money.

The word related to money here is *mammon*. Mammon was the currency of a kingdom. It was specifically related to money that was used to imperialize or capitalize on something that would sustain the consumerist whims of those who controlled their kingdoms. Mammon has an essence of being a "god" or idol, and thus people who put their trust in it are those who have lost control because they give control over to mammon.

So, in this passage Jesus makes as clear a

prophetic call as you can hear about how money is going to work in his kingdom, and the point needs no commentary. If you want to serve God with your life, you cannot serve your own interests, pad your wallets, put away enough to render faith irrelevant, or build your own kingdom. God's kingdom has, and always will, operate on the principle of manna, not mammon. God will always provide for his people as they do his work his way.

Judas, having grown up hustling and scalping, conniving and working the system, had learned that any gain can be justified as long as you don't go overboard. Daily survival was everyone's battle and it wasn't that strange for someone to skim a little out of the kitty as long as they generally did well. Judas had done well, but he had gotten used to viewing his time with Jesus and working for Jesus as a means of personal survival. The daily justification eventually created a habit, the pure voices became more silent, and the dangerous voices won out. Finally, in his final act, he sells out Jesus for a paycheck. The kiss of death!

His story is our story. No one means to use Jesus for his or her own gain, but the line between faithfully trusting God with manna almost always moves to mammon. This is why Paul also said to watch out for people who use the gospel for their own gain. "Unlike so many, we do not peddle the word of God for profit. On the contrary, in Christ we speak before God with sincerity, like men sent from God" (2 Corinthians 2:17). What did Paul mean by "pedal"? Well, again, simply that people kept their own kingdom moving forward by means of the gospel message.

You can't build two kingdoms at the same time. God's kingdom doesn't operate on the world's kingdom principles. This goes for both the ministry professional and any normal professional. This is an issue of discipleship, not churchmanship.

De-consumerizing the kingdom

Consumerism is based on mammon, not manna, and is both the fault of those who start and perpetuate the system as well as those who love the way the system serves them. Quoting from our book, *AND: the gathered and scattered church,*

> Consumerism is the self-focused drive to get as much as I can get with the least amount of effort. It coercively shifts the church away from its true call, from valuing giving to getting. It compels us to protect what we already have and only to give away what has become useless to

us. It erodes our sense of duty, honor, loyalty, and chivalry to live for the right things and the best things. It gets in the way of leaving a legacy for those behind us because it waters down our present understanding of what it means to follow Christ today. It pushes responsibility and expectations onto others instead of self and exchanges true spiritual formation for ankle-deep personal devotionals and self-help measures.

As you think about the church's decline, one positive way to think about it is in terms of discipleship instead of church attendance or church growth. The latter two measurements are what got us into this mess. Discipleship, on the other hand, forces us to ask the right questions and look at the real issues. There's simply no way to create discipleship around obedience, faith, kingdom risk, simplicity, and sacrifice while you try to keep life safe for people, or people safe in their lives. Regardless of whether you are presently making an income from the ministry, we all need to push against feeding people that want to be fed through mammon. Like God challenged the Israelites, we have to teach them to live day by day, in full faith, banking their very lives on the character of God to provide for them while they serve him.

Mammon-less tithe

Sadly, even our teaching on the tithe has been based on mammon theology and practice. Because we have created a consumer system and we need people to give to the system to fund the programs and our own livelihood, we have misrepresented the very heart of Old Testament tithing and New Testament giving. The real story of the tithe is that God's people consolidated their personal giving and only about ten percent was raked off the top for the religious leaders. The rest was distributed to the poor. The tithe and its effects on the world were awesome. It displayed God's heart for the people and kept a reasonable balance for those who made some portion of their living from working around the Temple.

This story of the tithe is not our present day story. Most churches rake off ten percent max for the poor and use the remaining ninety percent for in-house needs like pastoral salaries and building costs. We have a mammon tithe. We accept people's giving and use it for our own systems, creating a pesky need to keep spinning the plate or passing it! To recover the truest beauty of people's giving and the provision for those who make their living from the gospel, we need to model, teach, and make available the possibility of giving and receiving based on manna. Manna-based discipleship means that we have to teach the full tithe, full steward-ship, and let it be fully released to the world. And this can only be done as we lean our lives and structures into God and let him call us to be disci-ples instead of consumers. A bi-vocational network of leaders allows this process to happen a little bit easier.

From here on out, we're going to move beyond the prophetic call to the practical nature of making church cheaper and freeing up your life in the process. It's time to get nimble and have some fun! (By the way, I realize that the word "cheap" may make it sound "cheapened," but that is not what I mean. Keep in mind that I am simply referring to the actual financial and time costs associated with operating in different ways.)

Questions that might change your life

1. Why do you think Judas would have sold out Jesus for money? Where do you find yourself in his dilemma?

2. What would you stop doing for God if you didn't receive any financial benefit or pride

from it? What might God be saying to you about your motivations for serving him?

3. Is your financial ethos and practice both at a personal and ministry level based on manna or mammon?

A Story of How Church Just Happened

Cheap Beginnings

I'm not sure if you've ever seen the movie *Armageddon*. It's a Bruce Willis flick about a band of complete knuckleheads who end up saving the world. As the movie begins, they take fifteen minutes just to show you the individual characters in their own world. Although they all have unique and needed skills, they also have some serious flaws and, left to their own devices, would not amount to much. Yet together, they help each other through a myriad of moral weaknesses, short-sighted wisdom, and unforeseen struggles, and as in all good movies, they save the universe in the end.

That sort of sounds like Jesus with his twelve compadres. Unlike our present day analysis and recruitment of the A-team, Jesus seemed to prefer to work with the D-team. Unlike the insecure rabbis who tended to draw soft-skinned students that loved to spend years growing in their knowledge of concepts about God, Jesus drew leather-skinned laborers who were more attuned to active apprenticeship than mental accent or church attendance. This has not only been my story, but it has been the story of our church, and I want to unpack a little of our ecclesial journey so you can begin to think outside the box you may be in or are about to start to build. Here is a quick run-down of the main characters and how we have formed a bi-vocational network of incarnational communities while God built His church. We've had a significant influence on many people and we've had a lot of fun doing it together. As I share the story, realize we are only ten years into this mission so we hope you'll hold our story loosely like we do. We don't know what will happen in the next ten years, but we believe that our story can serve as a guide to those who want to see Jesus change the world through His church of normal people.

Hugh & Cheryl (me & my lady)

As I did my first church plant in Portland, about one third of my income came from personal missionary support, while the other two-thirds came from house painting. Because of our son's epilepsy, my wife Cheryl has never been able to work until about five years ago. Now, about nine years into the church life, I receive one third of my income from Adullam, one third from speaking and training other church leaders, and one third from Cheryl's real-estate career. Over the nine years Adullam has been a church, I have averaged about twenty-five hours a week for the actual church leadership roles. The rest of my time has been spent on the road, training leaders or painting as it was in the early days.

Matt & Maren

Matt was my original partner with both the church and with our national ministry platform called Missio. Matt worked with FedEx one third of the time, worked at a golf course for five dollars an hour, and had another one third of his income come from missionary support. As the church grew, Matt replaced his FedEx job with a one-third time stipend from the church and pieced the rest of his income together between church, training, and coaching. Two years ago, Matt gave up his church stipend and set out to start a small but successful publishing company. He remains one of our "elders" and continues to give Adullam about fifteen hours a week as a volunteer. His wife Maren has decided to stay home and be a mom.

Lou & Kim

Lou was one of our younger leaders that we tried to get on full time with Adullam in the early days. We had him raise support, but it didn't go very well. Adullam was about to try to throw a few thousand at Lou as a stipend, but instead Lou chose to sell medical equipment and now sells insurance. He was very successful and now seven years in, Lou is one of our "elders" and gives about fifteen hours a week to Adullam, and we are helping him get through seminary. Kim works part-time selling medical equipment and is transitioning more to home life as they just had their second son.

Greg & Becky

These two are book agents and writers but emerged as key lay leaders, pastoring almost one third of our congregation with marriage issues. They serve on our leadership council and continue to give about twenty hours a week to the pastoral needs of the congregation without any pay.

Curt & Shelley

Happily, Curt and Shelley joined Adullam about three years ago. They share their own house staging business and because of the success, Curt is able to serve on our main ministry team, giving about twenty hours a week to Adullam. His role has transitioned this last year into "do all the stuff no one else wants to do" and it's been so important, we are presently considering giving Curt a $2000 a month stipend just to say thanks!

Matt & Tonia

Just newly married Matt transitioned almost full-time missionary support from another para-church ministry to our network which has allowed Matt to focus on building his own community. He also serves in a training capacity for our city-wide network. Tonia is a full-time nurse.

Jason & Sue

While Sue is a part-time nurse, Jason has been our worship leader for nine years. He's been a poker dealer and administrative assistant most of the time, but has served Adullam faithfully for about

$300 a month. That means he's been working for a decade at the cost of what a normal worship leader earns in one year.

Mark & Stephanie/Johnny & Whitney

These two couples interned as church plant residents at Adullam, were able to raise some denominational and private funding from another congregation, but also chose to take the bi-vocational option. Mark painted houses and took a management position at a local mattress store while his wife started a home staging company. Jonny started an NGO called Artists for Denver that helps connect local musicians with foster care kids to give them music lessons. His wife Whitney also works full time in education. They both serve in a worship/arts capacity for Adullam.

Tim and Leslie

Tim moved to Denver from Baltimore and brought his mortgage banking business with him. Initially we asked Tim to serve an administrative pastoral role and offered him $2000 a month. Because of the success of his business he offered to give up his stipend and continues to serve on our ministry team without pay. Leslie is a nurse and they just had their first child.

So that is our D-team (my A-team) after nine years on the ground. Besides these core leaders, we have many others who have led worship, handled the children's ministry, and run the general church administration, but most have never taken more than a small $300-500 stipend. As we've all committed to modeling and expanding this bi-vocational network of leaders, we are seeing fruit both in our ministries and in our lives. We are a network of incarnational communities around Denver, and between the two congregational sites, we oversee about 400 people. It's not a huge story, but I think you'll agree it is a healthy one. Most leaders would love to live this way and have this level of influence without killing themselves, overworking, or having to be the one single leader that everyone expects to hang the moon. Like Bruce Willis's band of jack-wagons, we all play to our strengths, no one cares about titles or personal success, and God has built his church.

Cheap Story (The nutshell version)

> *IMAGINE . . . What would happen if people came together to commit to one another, to mutually discover what God's work in them*

looked like, and pressed ahead to do God's work in their world? Imagine the profound meaning people could find for themselves— and their spiritually hungry friends—who want to re-orient around something real. Welcome to the family we call "Adullam." We are a peculiar community of blessing and acceptance. Our purpose is to retell the story of Christ through community, commu- nion, and mission. We are seeking to adjust our lives around life, mission, and teachings of Jesus Christ in the hopes that our experi- ence will bring into clear focus this real and living Person to anyone watching. We are not a place to go, but a people to belong to—a people who have been called to live out the Good News of God's Kingdom in every niche of culture.

This vision statement was made in year two of our story. If you ever want to read the full version, check out *The Tangible Kingdom*. Here is the nutshell version. A group of friends (six in all) moved to Denver to create a missions community focused on living out and making tangible the kingdom of God. Since Jesus called the kingdom "good news," we thought that if we could experience it and make it accessible to others, everything else would take care of itself. And it did. We often say, "And church just happened."

We had a simple kingdom DNA (communion/community/mission) that we lived out through intentional weekly and monthly rhythms. Everyone worked a normal job and as the first house filled with new friends and people who were finding faith, we just kept going. We "housed" the DNA in what we called incarnational communities and began reproducing them around town. Now after nine years, we have communities spanning forty-five miles, and nothing has changed. We teach the same DNA, we put people in the same environment for the DNA, people find we truly are good news, and we grow. We added weekly or bi-monthly congregational gatherings and have found the interplay between our scattered presence and our gathered presence to work beautifully. We still have no staff serving more than twenty-five hours a week. We structure a bi-vocational leadership model and people serve the movement in their gifting based on APEST (Ephesians 4). There are no titles, no hard and fast roles, just people banding together to live well and serve well. We've never had a church fight or church split, and whereas many people have come to "check us out" and leave because it was a bit too weird, the ones who have remained would never trade it for anything. Our budget to run the entire mess is about $12,000-15,000 a month, (approximately one-sixth) of what we found many churches operate on. The combined leadership team is still having a blast and we think our story could open up a new world for thousands of people who have tasted the bitterness of both church and professional ministry.

The rest of this book will unpack this story a bit more so that you can find some new possibilities for your own life, calling, and even your church.

Warning: Don't just think about church. Think about your life. This happened through normal peasants! Gifted, serious, intentional, people of high character, well-educated, well-versed in ministry, *but* we all worked normal jobs. So, try to find yourself in our story.

Questions that might change your life

1. If you could find a handful of committed BiVo friends to help guide communities and lead a congregation, would you enjoy this picture of life? What stands in the way of this happening?

2. Make a list of what it would take to get to this picture? What things are out of your

control that you can give to God and what things are in your control to change? Start with what you can do.

Cheap Church Uncracked

You probably have a few questions after my quick summary in the previous chapter, so now let's crack open this nut and the nutcakes that lived this way to see if we can find some points of connection to you and your story. As we walk backward looking at how God can grow a strong church from normal people, consider the three leverage points again and begin to rethink your life.

Cheap DNA

In Matthew 16, Jesus tells Peter that he will now build his church upon him. If I were Peter and feeling more than a little sketchy about what the church really is and how to get there, I'd want to know a few more details: "That's great Jesus, I'd love to see you build your church around my life, but what should I do? Do you want me to strike up the band and do one of those attractional, program-centered churches, or maybe go smaller, like maybe house church? Should we be missional, mega, or micro? Do you want me to be a network of cell gatherings or should we just set up camp down by the Temple and start some outdoor gatherings? Maybe we'd put on some cool skits about Nero, hand out bread, and whatever?"

It's normal for church leaders to want to have a vision and clear pathway to realize it, but Jesus offers an alternative, "I will give you the keys to the kingdom." He's not going to give us the keys to our church, or the keys to growing a church or starting one or even fixing one. He's not going to give us the manual on social justice, helping the poor, spiritual formation, or making disciples. Instead, he gives us the keys to the kingdom, which if we take it seriously, will produce fruit in everything else. Best news of all . . . Jesus does the work of building. All we have to do is live the kingdom! Now that should calm you down as long as you really want Jesus to build something. You don't have to have the master vision, but you do have to be clear on what is the kingdom DNA.

In *The Tangible Kingdom*, we studied every passage where Jesus talked or modeled the kingdom and it seemed as those attributes fit neatly into three spheres of kingdom life.

Communion

Those things we do to help connect people verti-cally with the Spirit of God (*communal worship, teaching through scripture, liturgical practice, development of devotional life, Christian fellowship, Lord's supper*).

Inclusive Community

How we connect saints and sojourners together as we create a place of belonging for everyone without judgment or weird spiritual overtones (*creating neutrally safe social environments—be it a party in a home, going out together for dinner, a movie, concert, or watching a child's tee ball game).*

Mission

As James 1:27 says, "pure religion" is found in meeting practical needs. We are a "sent" people on mission, but our mission is to bless people, and blessing in the truest sense is to bring social, spiritual, and physical help in order that all of life can be redeemed (*We do this by finding needs and meeting them as soon as possible. These spiritual, social, or physical needs cost time and money, and we try to be a blessing in the most spontaneous ways that God leads our communities to be*).

As we stated in *The Tangible Kingdom*, we find that whenever you get a few friends together, or an entire community that learns to intentionalize their weekly and monthly rhythms around communion/community/mission, the kingdom becomes tangible, good news naturally draws people, and God builds his church. What's nice about focusing on the kingdom DNA is that it can be done by anyone. You don't need to pay anyone to do it. It can happen without a building or a staff team or a program. It's completely free of charge. Sure, it does cost time and can cost money as God leads you to bless and include other people, but there's no infrastructure cost.

Cheap environments

Jesus was brilliant. He not only gave us an inexpensive and easily reproducible kingdom DNA, he also gave us nimble structures or "environments" by which the DNA could be moved into the culture. This idea of "nimbility" really came from looking at the structure of an incarnational community.

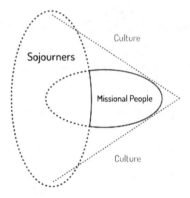

Many of us know "church" to be the place to go for spiritual services. In most cities, churches are stable places that don't move. They can't move because of the brick and mortar building as well as the staffing structure that stays put and asks people to "come to us." This is why it's called *attractional church*. Others have also called this structure of church *extractional* because it teaches people to leave the world and come to the building for spiritual food. It is not a nimble structure in any way.

And because it stays put, it ends up costing a lot more than it should, only delivering the communion circle in the diagram above, leaving two thirds of the gospel out of the equation. It therefore ends up being bad news instead of good news. Spiritually, when Christians only focus on their formation (vertically) without forming through inclusive community and blessing (horizontally), their extracted lifestyle produces a subtle but sinister problem called the leaven of the Pharisees. That's bad news! What's even more discouraging is that most churches spend over eighty-five percent of their combined time and financial resources propping up this Pharisee factory.

Jesus, of course, not only removed the need for the Temple, Temple priests, and Temple worship, he warned spiritual leaders to "watch out for the leaven of the Pharisee." In other words, Jesus would have challenged this consumeristic system that costs a ton but delivers very little of the kingdom.

So Jesus not only gave us the "keys to the kingdom," he also gave us a cheap environment called an incarnational community that would be the new substructure on which he would build his church. The incarnational community could function from the context of a home, out in a public zone, under a tree, or inside a synagogue. This structure would not be brick and mortar, but instead would be based on people and thus able to move, morph, easily reproduce, and grow without any costs. It not only moves because it is people rather than a building, but also it can now deliver or inject the culture with all three circles of kingdom DNA.

I said "substructure" instead of full structure for one reason. Each individual community can be considered a "church." In fact, in New Testament times the church was just a network of these smaller house churches. As persecution forced God's burgeoning church to be mobile, Christianity spread past the Jewish culture and their synagogue or temple-based gathering and the church most often operated as a loose, but connected, kingdom network. That's why the letters were written to the church in Corinth, or the church in Smyrna, and so on.

Theologically, I agree that a band of friends under one roof is the church, but we've found it more practical to call it an individual incarnational community, and create a large "church" vision for how they network and play together for a larger kingdom function. This is why we call Adullam "A congregational network of incarnational communities." The individual community, therefore, is the primary organizing structure of the movement instead of the building, the weekend services, and the staff.

So now we have a cheap kingdom DNA and a cheap structure or environment out which the DNA can live its good news. To say it another way, the structure of an incarnational community is an intentional group of people who live out three circles of kingdom DNA and who provide a place of non-judgmental belonging for spiritually disoriented god-seekers. There's no need to try to attract people to a place because the people themselves are attractive. There's no need to program anyone into anything because we invite people to join us in kingdom activity. The culture around us loves to be included and they love to bless others, so two thirds of the kingdom DNA meshes beautifully with the values of the culture. And as they move toward missional people and experience the good news, they will eventually come to faith in the King of this kingdom.

Cheap process

When the DNA doesn't cost and the environment or structures that you use to get the DNA into the culture don't cost, then the congregational structures are also far less costly.

In our story, we decided to let God build his

church through a natural process we call "missional flow," which simply means a natural way of living life in the kingdom that ends up eventually forming a congregation.

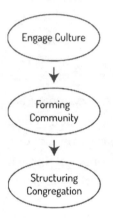

You can read more about how to do this in *AND*, but essentially we begin by engaging culture with the good news. We of course focus on two of the three circles the most (inclusive community/mission) since they are culture-friendly. We party all the time, we have many comfy social environ-ments without any weird spiritual overtones, and we help everyone we can with anything that comes up. In the engaging culture season (which never ends), we focus on making friends, learning their stories, letting them know ours, and including them in two circle kingdom experiences.

In our story, people did move toward us, and eventually some even came to faith. Thus we naturally moved to the second aspect of Forming Community. This was done by simply adding the third circle of communion—an informal time around scripture, prayer, Christian dialogue, and discipleship.

Neither engaging culture nor forming community cost much at all. The best news about that is that anyone can be involved, so there's no financial risk associated with getting God's people to live on mission and live out kingdom principles within the context of missional community. There's literally no down side!

Most churches and even church plants have a very high up-front cost, as the diagram shows. The idea in the past has been that if we front the money, we'll get the desired result, which is a self-supportive congregation. Most church plants get about two to three years up-front money with the expectation that they will be self-sustaining. But it doesn't happen that easy.

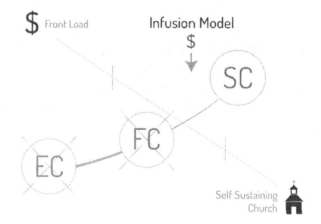

The old funding model, shown above and going from high left to low right, is incredibly risky and also limits who and how many can play. For instance, one denomination we were working with sent out forty new church plant teams, gave them each $250,000, and within five years had only one success story. That's $10,000,000 down the ol' church hole! More painful than the statistics are the 120 marriages that were deeply tested, 120 leaders who now question their own calling, and some who have left the ministry all together. There's a lot at stake when you put money before mission.

In our story, we started with no money, and therefore no pressure, and in the end enjoyed the process of watching God build something naturally. During the first twenty-four months we simply engaged the culture with practical blessing, parties, and deep relationships. Many people found faith and we began making disciples. Most importantly, as you can see from the diagram, it didn't cost anything other than time and relationship. Engaging culture is cheap!

We also began to multiply incarnational communities and noticed that cost has remained the same. Zero!

Here's the beautiful nugget of wisdom we learned. God has set up his mission to be completely free of charge for most of the process. Anyone can do it, in any context and, in a very real way, God's church doesn't really take any money. It can be made easier with money, and the scriptures show us that money is important, but we have to reframe this entire idea of church to be something God can build with very little, or at least a ton less than we spend on it.

So what about the money? When do you need it, or at least, when is it helpful? In our story, we began to feel a pinch as we faced the need to hold the communities together in one mission. In other words, as we began to structure the communities into congregation. Teaching, discipleship, evangelism, blessing, benevolence, fellowship, were all decentralized, but we still wanted to be together. We just didn't want it to cost too much.

We needed a little money to rent a space to gather everyone and we needed a little money to allow a few of us some extra time for leadership development, but that was about it. In other words, when you begin to congregationalize, or hold people and mission together, you may need a little money. We needed a few days off from our normal work because the time it took to help our leaders lead their own communities became too intense. We needed a little money to handle some administrative tasks, but that was about it.

It doesn't cost much to do inclusive community. It doesn't cost much to bless people, but it does cost something to bring God's people together for communion.

Making disciples is cheaper than making consumer Christians. Put another way, letting God build his church as we focus on the kingdom is much cheaper than trying to build church without the kingdom.

Cheaper transfer growth process

In addition to the process of getting people to engage the culture in communities, we also had to set up an internal process that would keep the transfer growth of non-missional, consumer-oriented Christians from "costing" us time and

Observance
Our story
Their Story

Preparation
Active Spiritual
Formation
(TK Primer)

Participation
Real Life Practice

Partnership
Leadership &
Ownership

eventually money. This process is outlined in detail in *AND*, but the short version is that we provided quarterly training opportunities for new people that tested their resolve on the front end before we gave them much of our valuable time. Of course many people have left because we didn't "plug them in" immediately or make them feel all snug and comfy, but this process is critical if you are serious about giving your best time to what produces your best fruit.

Questions that might change your life

1. As you see this alternative picture of church, what resonates or seems attractive to you?
2. What parts of this story scare you or cause some trepidation?
3. Do you see ways to synthesize some of these cheaper aspects into your present structure and rhythms of church, or do you think you'd have to start over completely?

Full-Time Futility

Last year, I was with Mike Breen, founder and director of 3dm, enjoying some golf, and boating around the intercoastal area of South Carolina. But my favorite time was discussing the feudal system of ministry he came out of in northern England. The feudal system is essentially where church leaders are paid by the highest hierarchical point of an institutional church. Just like in the Anglican or Catholic churches and a good number of Protestant denominations as well, it doesn't matter if your church is growing or pathetically dwindling down to fifteen people. You get paid what you get paid. Feudal isn't the same as futile, but it sometimes produces the same fruit.

As we have talked about a cheaper church based on individual people banding together in intentional mission, and that these people are working normal, nominal jobs, you can see it is in stark contrast to a system of futility where leaders do all the work for consumers. Disciples get made in the first model whereas you tend to produce church attenders in the second. And since church attenders don't create disciples, it's a futile process.

I know it's a paradigm-buster, but history shows us that the gospel got around the world primarily through unpaid saints. There have always been state-paid priests, monastics, and spiritual leaders who have lived lives completely focused on the gospel, but until about 100-200 years ago, the support of spiritual leaders was pretty minimal at best. The picture of a pastor being fully funded, with bennies, a parsonage, and fifty hours a week to completely focus on ministry ventures is really quite strange. If you were to ask Moses, Abraham, Elijah, Jesus, Paul, or the millions of men and women who gave their lives for the gospel, very few would speak of being safe and secure within the constructs of our modern day ministry provision. It's time to leave the futility of feudal church leadership and financial structures and free the church to the peasant leaders.

Free labor force

In Matthew 9:35-38 we read,

> Jesus went through all the towns and villages, teaching in their synagogues, proclaiming the good news of the kingdom and healing every disease and sickness. When he saw the crowds, he had compassion on them, because they were harassed and helpless, like sheep without a shepherd. Then he said to his disciples, "The harvest is plentiful but the workers are few. Ask the Lord of the harvest, therefore, to send out workers into his harvest field."

Interestingly, as Jesus got emotional about the fact that people don't have folks to guide them spiritually, he didn't ask them to pray for full-time pros, seminary grads, or pontiffs. He wanted simple laborers and faithful workers. Jesus knew that there were simply too many people for just a few paid leaders to handle. So Jesus gave us hope for the whole world based on normal people getting into the field.

God has gifted the body with leadership gifts that are there to equip normal people to do the work of ministry. That means that the actual ministers are unpaid saints and that the actual work of building God's church comes through the head, heart, and hands of the average Joe or Jolene. Amazingly, God promises to build his church on the volunteer work of real people who live sacred lives with secular provision. Kingdom DNA is cheap, kingdom environments called "incarnational communities" are cheap, and people who work with God are cheap.

Cheap laborers

As I looked at this heading, "cheap laborers," I have to admit—it looks as if we are suggesting that we use people for building our kingdoms, or maybe even that Jesus is suggesting that we use people to build his kingdom. Nothing could be further from the truth. The fact of the matter is that people find meaning when they are used by God. There's nothing that encourages, inspires, or propels people into spiritual growth more than being used in God's kingdom plan. In other words, helping people discover life's meaning is cheap, and we should never feel bad about moving the ministry from the hands of the pros into the lives of the common saint. The way someone finds the sacred is when they see God use their secular vocation and lot in life.

My favorite masters of uniting the sacred and secular were the Trappist Monks. Saint Benedict began this monastic movement in the sixth century. His motto was *ora et labora* which is Latin for *pray and work*. Amidst many other monastic orders that asked and sometimes begged for financial support, the Trappists were known for being self-sufficient communities. Unlike some monastic communities that lived far away from the local city center, Trappists often lived out their cloistered life in close proximity to town so that their products would be a blessing to people and so that they could sustain their own calling to pray and work. They baked bread, crafted beer, raised livestock, and hosted guests like any other modern day resort. Apparently about twenty to thirty percent of the entire economic output in medieval times came from their agricultural and creative enterprises. Amazingly, at the time of the Reformation, a third of all the land in England was owned by these sacred secularists! Rodney Stark in a book called, *The Victory of Reason: How Christianity Led to Freedom, Capitalism, and Western Success*, said that capitalism was invented in monasteries in the ninth, tenth, and eleventh centuries. The reason was that these men (as opposed to the greedy, self-oriented society) actually believed God was letting them steward his resources and took the call to bless people and create sustainable products in line with God's heart for them. They maintained integrity, compassion, creativity and hard work . . . and it changed the world.

Again, not all monastic orders have such a high value for work. The Franciscans and Dominicans, like Buddhist monks, have to depend upon charity, donations, who are "set apart" and will be provided for. Again, I don't think it's helpful to dissuade people from being dependent upon others, but as you consider your own calling, I want you to be aware that there are options. Missiology requires that we ask, "Based on the world as it exists today, with the unique economic, social, global issues facing people, what is my best response and option for blessing people and sustaining my life?" I believe in most centuries, as in the time we live in today, those that take the Trappist approach may enjoy life and do more good than those who wait on others to empower their passion.

Waking up the body

To me, this is one of the most exciting opportunities the present day dilemmas are opening up for us. People will come alive when you give them a vision for uniting their daily work with God's daily work. Like waking up after a long slumber, God's church is everywhere made up of people who live in strategic neighborhoods; who have strategic jobs and public profile; who know what would bless a community and how to use their networks, resources, relational pull, and unique skills to see God's kingdom break through. People have good reason to be bored stiff through weekly church attendance, but if you can help people find out why they are a plumber or teacher, lawyer or Starbucks barista, and then give them a reason to wake up prayerfully and expectantly to see God use them, it will ignite spiritual fervor you can never muster up through a sermon or worship set.

Adullam operates around an Old Testament concept called *tsaddiqim*. This is a Hebrew word that means *the Righteous*. Specifically, it refers to people who follow God and bring blessing, or *shalom*, to a city. Proverbs 11:10 reads, "When the righteous prosper, the city rejoices." As Jesus brings the reality of a new kingdom into the kingdom of darkness in this world, God's people stand out because as they prosper, the whole city prospers. There's no individualized evangelical faith within the *tsaddiqim*, but instead a community of Jesus followers that place the foci of their personal faith squarely on the idea of together being stewards of God's kingdom resources for the shalom of the people around them.

This is why we call everyone to the BiVo life and why we think the church made up of BiVo's is a better option for the masses. God's people are made to work, and they love to work, so let's help them know how. Everything is sacred, even driving a beer truck for Coors!

Equipping gets more done than doing

If we view every person as a missionary and only pay those who spend the majority of their time modeling, equipping, and holding God's people together in mission, then the most costly aspect of ministry is time. And time, like any other resource, can be used as mammon or manna. It can be an idol that restricts our movement or a daily provision we use to leverage for God.

One Sunday in Adullam, I addressed how our time is worth as much as our money. In fact, even as our money has been made an idol, so we've made an idol of our time. I got a lot of scrunched brows. "Here's how I know we have made our calendar our idol. None of you ever RSVP when we ask for it." More furrowed brows stared back at me. "When you don't RSVP, you're essentially saying that you don't want to commit to anyone or anything 'just in case' something better might come up. In other words, your time has become something you use for yourself instead of for others. It's not a time management issue. It's a gospel issue."

Whenever I train people or pastors on incarnational/missional living, the biggest questions I get are about time. How do we add incarnational life to our already jammed schedules? Pastors who justify their own salaries often say, "Our people don't have the time to do this and that's why they have to hire me and my staff. We're set apart so that we can do what they can't." The pace of our world is, for sure, too fast and our people can barely Sabbath, let alone give up their last few minutes to others. Shouldn't we prioritize our families if we have few moments to spare?

To answer this, we have to see it at the level of idolatry. There is a heart issue in every person that we simply have to call out. But in addition to the "air war" of training and speaking prophetically to our people, we have to teach them that incarnational life doesn't have to be an additional time constraint. We have to help them see the potential and the opportunities all around them. God designed his people to do the work of ministry and everyone can be at least a part-time missionary.

Here's a little grid I use to show people the missional possibilities of their lives.

- How many hours do you spend on the

athletic field sidelines, in the gym, or at the school watching your kids play sports? The average parent spends *ten hours a week* with the same parents and the same kids.

- How many of your twenty-one meals a week do you eat out, either for lunch break, or coffee before or after work, or for dinner out? Most say four to eight. If each are roughly an hour, that's another *five hours a week.*
- How many meals do you eat at home that you could invite someone else to share? Most say two. So that's another *four hours.*
- How often do you work out or do recreational activities a week? Most say *five hours a week.*

As you can see, just in these basic activities we do every week, almost any person can be a twenty to twenty-five hour a week missionary. Missional life isn't adding anything, but it is seeing everywhere you are as a possible mission field.

Now, if we can give our people vision for their mission field, it exposes the fact that we may not need to hire anyone full time to do the work of ministry. The synergy of God's inexpensive mission happens when you, as a part-time or even unpaid pro, spend the majority of your time equipping the people of God for the mission of God.

Cheap leaders

It always sounds inspirational to talk about releasing God's people to do the work of ministry until that reality requires that leaders let go. The fact of the matter is that getting God's labor force moving is super cheap, but it only happens if our present leadership paradigm changes from being doers of ministry to becoming equippers of the ministry. In other words, the more you equip, the cheaper church will be. The more you keep doing the work, the more expensive church will be.

God does call some to be leaders among all the workers. And both Jesus and Paul allow for some to be set apart and given compensation for their unique work. But the equation breaks down when we think our calling means that we get to do the work of ministry instead of equipping others. Here's the bottom line: Making a living from the gospel should be for those who are equipping people to do the actual work. Ephesians 4 gives us the primary framework for how God provides leadership functions (not positions) that propel God's people to do the heavy lifting. Most of us grew up believing that our jobs were to be the pastor, or the evangelist, or the teacher. Often, I've even heard people say, "I'm the teaching pastor" or I'm the senior pastor" as if these are positions to be filled and paid for. But the scriptures don't support this. Instead, Paul lays out the ministry or leadership functions that are gift-based with the clear understanding that they are to train others to do the teaching, the pastoring, the evangelism, etc.

I'm not sure how we missed this, but it has created an incredible financial burden upon local congregations. It has created a false sense of security and sense of false worth for many leaders as well as creating and propping up a consumer culture in our congregations where God's people expect us to do the work for them. They miss out on their own calling and we cheapen ours.

Should people get paid for leading? Yes, but we have to rethink this and make sure that, if we do take a stipend or a salary, then most of our time is used for training and leadership development of the congregation. Even though Adullam is not focused on the Sunday gathering, we still find that when we offer a church service weekly, people naturally sit down to be served. Last year, we made a significant adjustment by adding what we call, "Wild Goose Sunday." Once a month, we unplug the speakers, rally people for a simple communion in the sanctuary, and then break them up into training rooms. Each room is about equipping. The people immediately changed. When they know they are about to be equipped, they cease looking to be served and they get ready to go serve others. Just this monthly small shift helped us strengthen our workers and corrected our course back toward mission.

Because we decentralize teaching, shepherding, evangelism, to our scattered incarnational communities in Adullam, we don't have to hire teaching pastors, shepherds, or evangelists. We have seven people on part-time staff and the combined cost is $6500 a month. Because each person is spending their time equipping, we get seven for the price of one, and the seven have a blast doing what they love and feel called to based on their gifting instead of being hired under the banner of "pastor" and try to do everything. We'll spend more time on the balance of decentralizing and centralizing in a minute, but don't miss this key: The people of God are your cheapest asset and they want to be leveraged.

Cheap movements

This is a good time to mention how movement really happens. Here's the simple reality: The kingdom cost God a lot, but the life of the kingdom is offered freely to all. Kingdom DNA lived out in nimble environments called incarnational communities will naturally develop disciples of the kingdom.

They will become good news and remain good news to the world. Those communities will grow and then form into congregational networks called churches. And as these churches continue the process, movement happens. A simple way to remember this is:

DNA >> Disciple >> Community >> Congregation >> Movement

Most denominations or networks feel that they simply don't have enough leaders to reach the culture, and it's true if you view the church in the old way. But if you view every disciple as a carrier for the DNA, then you have a built-in farm system and the clear makings of a movement. Leveraging the laity isn't just about growing your church. It's about releasing the potential for explosive movement. If you view people as Christians, converts, church attenders, or in view of membership, you'll settle for them to stay in those categories. But if you see every church attender as a potential kingdom disciple, and you structure your congregation to be a network of incarnational communities, who all live out *communion/community/mission* then movement is actually inevitable. You don't know if you'll reach 10,000,000 or 1,000, but if you focus on viewing church as a farm system of developing every Christ follower, something more than just a church will occur!

Questions that might change your life

1. Write down all the benefits to the disciple-making process you can imagine if you worked at least part-time like the people you serve.

2. In contrast, make a list of the struggles you think you might encounter by splitting your time and energy between two vocations.

3. What inspires you about the concept of being a modern day Trappist?

Cheap Gatherings

Jesus died for His Church. It cost Him every-thing and he purchased it by His own blood. And since he paid so much for it, it should also be darn expensive for us!

Because the weekend church gathering is such a huge part of the traditional Christian experience, I wanted to give an entire chapter to it. Just like I am in favor of, but also leary about, people making a living from the gospel, I am likewise in favor of and scared to death of the benefits and pitfalls of the weekly church service.

I wrote an entire book on how the gath-ered and scattered church can work together, so if you want a more thorough explanation of how God has designed the church to operate, look for *AND: the gathered and scattered church*. The short version is this: God's people need to be together, and whether it is in a living room or filling a coliseum, there's nothing inherently wrong with scores of saints worshipping God, enjoying each other, and taking an hour break from their normal missionary life. But, if the average Christian is not living a missionary life, the church gathering can be like an anchor that drags a battleship to a halt, causing would-be revolutionaries to recline, pop the top of a cold one, tip the bill of their hat over their eyes, and sleepily drift with the rest of the culture.

So the issue is not whether we have a worship gathering, but why we have one, how we structure it to keep God's people on mission, and how to keep it from costing so much time, money, and energy. The key to this balance is found in the concept of true worship.

Consider this email exchange I had with a worship leader we'll call Wendy.

> *Hi Hugh, I just read your book Sacrilege, and I loved it! You mentioned that you don't like to sing in church, and as a worship leader, I found your reasoning to be quite intriguing.*

As I've read many recent missional books, I'm really struggling with the role of music, worship in general, and how this fits into my calling to lead people toward God. I'm at a bit of a loss, can you help? —Wendy

My response:

Wendy, Yes, in Sacrilege I did mention that I have never really enjoyed singing in church. Other than singing an occasional Black Keys song while riding my Harley, I'm really not into singing at all, anywhere. But as I've processed my aversion, I've come to realize that it's not about the singing. It's about the worship. Real worship.

Just a few weeks ago, I was speaking at the largest missional community conference called Verge. Verge is hosted by Austin Stone, and with Aaron Ivey leading the worship, even I couldn't help but enjoy the attempt at vocal engagement! A few days later, I spoke at Austin New Church, pastored by Brandon Hatmaker and again, I completely dug the artistically beautiful and authentic worship. I actually sang at both events. Not loud, but a few squeaks came out.

So what's the real issue?

It's not that I don't want to sing. It's that I don't want to sing with people that JUST sing!

Verge is a gathering of paid and peasant saints who are all living against the grain of consumer-church and consumer Christianity and living deep lives of sacrifice, missional community, ministry to the poor, the lost, and the least. ANC is also a unique church as told in a book called The Barefoot Church. *They began simply by serving the poor. In both cases, the church leaders that come, and the regular folks who attend, are not trying to grow their churches or prop up the show. In fact, they are all against the show. Instead, they are learning to live a real story of daily worship. They are trying to balance both worship as a vertical event with worship as a horizontal lifestyle.*

Jesus said, "Love the Lord your God with all your heart, mind, soul, and strength," (vertical), "AND love your neighbor as much as you love yourself" (horizontal).

In other words, worship on Sunday is only going to be as deep as our worship the rest of the week. Depth through song, liturgy, spoken word, and preaching is only going to be as meaningful as the level of meaning we bring to others around us.

In fact, I'd submit that if we, as Romans 12:1 encourages, "present our bodies as living sacrifices, holy and pleasing to God, which is our spiritual act of worship," 24-7, we could come together on Sunday, bang wooden spoons on a garbage can and have an amazing time of worship. When God's people live large lives of kingdom good news, it makes sense to go vertical and get audible about our love for God. —Hugh.

Mammonless gatherings

So now you know, I don't mind singing. But for goodness sake, let's not let it cost so much! I think that was what Wendy was actually struggling through. Should she make a living helping people go vertical if they don't have much horizontal going on? If it's true that most churches spend the majority of their staff time and resources providing a worship and teaching gathering, is it possible to adjust the amount of time and resources we give it to fit the actual fruit we get from it?

I think it's a hard question to give a black and white answer for, but here a few things we can know for sure.

First, the worship we live out as missional people can be done for free, so most of our worship shouldn't cost a dime.

Second, God does like his people to go vertical. The scriptures are full of references to the power of gathering in order to lift up Jesus through song, cymbals, or choir bells. It's just there, all over the place, so it doesn't seem fair to suggest we unplug the entire show.

Third, we should shoot for balance, not purity on either side. Instead of reacting too harshly or too quickly, consider splitting the cost, at least. If you spend $75,000 on a worship leader and $120,000 on a building for people to gather vertically in, then put the same amount of money into serving the poor, equipping people to go out in missional communities, or simply giving the money away to smaller church plants that can't even afford to buy a portable Bose sound system.

Fourth, determine in your own life if you'd feel better serving with your gifts for free. I've found worship leaders who make $100,000 a year and some who do the same job for a weekly Starbucks gift card. I think the choice is personal, and if you'd have more fun giving your gift away, I'd encourage you to do it. Personally, I believe anyone making a living from gospel ministry should only get paid if they are equipping more and more people to do what they do. So if a leader takes a full salary and is creating and developing others, dandy! But woe to any leader, pastor, teacher, or worship leader who doesn't think this through with an eye to fighting consumerism and bringing balance to vertical and horizontal worship.

Balancing the gathering and scattering

Before we go into specifics of how to do this, on the next page there is a grid we use to help churches decide what to spend money on. This is Adullam's present grid of what we centralize and what we decentralize.

You'll see that in Adullam, as we see in many missional churches, most of the work of ministry is decentralized to the volunteer core we call "the people of God." Because the missional community becomes the primary organizing structure of

"CHEAP"

What is Decentralized

Community
Cultural Engagement
Evangelism
Teaching
Accountability
Crisis Management
Youth Ministry
Sheep Herding
Mission to the "poor"

Giving

What is Centralized

Worship - "Vertical"
Corporate Community
Vision
Training / Equipping
Children's Ministry

**"COMES WITH
A COST"**

the church instead of the Sunday church gathering,
God's missionary people can handle most of the
load. The key to remember is that the more you
decentralize to missional communities, the cheaper
your gatherings will be. You really only need to pay
for what you centralize, so think it through and
make sure there's a specific reason you need to
gather that is different from what your people experience when they scatter into communities.

We decentralize shepherding, teaching, crisis
intervention, pastoral care, community, evangelism, discipleship, giving, social action, blessing,
and discipleship of our children. That means we
don't have to pay for a teaching pastor, discipleship
pastor, missions pastor, or children's pastor.

We centralize vision, corporate worship and communion, training, some of the giving, and connection for our kids. Thus we do have to pay minimally for a gathering space in which to do this, and some part-time staff to help equip the congregation to do all the decentralized stuff.

Again, because we see our missional communities as the main thing, we find incredible nimbility and stability, and everything gets done for a fraction of the cost. Several friends of mine pastor large churches in Denver. During a recent snowstorm, one of the mega churches had to cancel their Sunday services. So did we. A few days later, I called Tony and asked him what closing down for week did to them as a church. "Well, it was a great break for me personally, but it will take the church at least six months to recover financially from losing one week's offering," Tony sheepishly revealed. He followed up with the same question to me. I replied, "Ya, I had a great day off too, but all I did was send a Facebook notice out that said, 'Enjoy the snow.'" Because we don't take our offering on Sunday but teach people to give silently through the mail or direct deposit, and because our communities still get together and have learned to do most of "church" outside of the church gathering, we not only survive a bad snowstorm, we enjoy it!

In-house or outhouse

As you consider our story, notice that there are many ways to spread the cost of time and resources around to people or outsource it altogether. Most churches hire a communications admin position because they used to have to send letters out to the congregation, folding letters, licking envelopes, and taking trips to the PO box. Now one person can in five minutes send a Facebook message or an email to everyone. Done! We used to have creative arts directors to make videos or spend time working with people to develop drama performances. Now we can just download cool YouTube videos that make the point.

We outsourced our nursery care through early toddlers to a babysitting service. It cost very little and gave our new moms a needed break. We also now outsource our financial services for church giving and year-end receipts, heavy counseling situations, and marriage retreats. I know it may seem weird. I've even heard of churches that literally outsource their bible teaching. They gather friends, download some Tim Keller or other well-known expositor, and away they go. It's not our cup of tea, but it is helpful to think outside the box for how you can get internal issues taken care of for a fraction of the cost.

Now let's turn our attention to the biggest cost of doing church—the church building itself.

Cheap spaces

On our way to a speaking engagement in Kansas City, my friend Lance told me about a young church planter who had an old historical stone church not only given to them, but also the money to completely renovate the building. "Hugh, I know you're not really big on buildings, but you're going to like this place," he said.

As we pulled up, I remember thinking, "Dang, that is pretty nice." We walked in and I went straight for the sanctuary, opening the beautiful, thick wood doors. I was completely silenced by the ornate, but simple majesty of the high domed ceilings, beautiful stained-glass windows, and the long, rounded pews. You could almost hear the angels singing. Lance said, "Pretty sweet, ay?" I looked at him and said, "I have building envy."

As we've talked about the trap of program-based, building-based ministry and the burden it places on everyone, we can still stop to appreciate the upside of buildings. We don't need buildings to find sacred space, but sacred buildings, even an empty cinderblock shell, can at times help out. As we left, I told Lance, "Look, it's not that I have anything against buildings, I just don't want to pay for one of them. If someone gave me this, I'd be a happy man!"

Some realities to consider about buildings

The cost of the building isn't just the cost of the building. In an article in Church Executive, August issue, 2011, the main point was that most of the costs of a building are the upkeep and the staffing required to keep things running. We've often thought of trying to purchase a cheap space, but it was the "other expenses" that scared us away, time and time again.

If you decide to live and share ministry with a handful of friends as we did, I'd caution you against ever owning anything unless, like this young planter, you're given the building, you're given the renovation, and you get at least a couple years cash cushion. Anything less will most likely pull your focus, concern, and actual time away from people. Here are a few points of wisdom for any facility considerations.

1. **You should rarely have to buy a building.** With the amount of churches closing, there is such a glut of vacant or barely used spaces, you should look for someone to give you one, or at least share one with you. Especially in large, urban spaces, the cities will often sell

you or lease for free old buildings they would love to see updated.

2. **Only purchase a multiple-use space.** If you were able to purchase a building you should only buy one that could be easily resold or reused for other purposes. An old historical space like I mentioned actually fits the bill because it can be sold or used for events such as weddings or even restaurants. In Scotland, the best pubs are actually old churches, and you'll see this trend emerge stateside as well.

3. **Never pay for office space.** Over the last eight years, we've rented for free, or nearly so, library conference rooms, back rooms of restaurants, seminary or college classrooms, hotel lobbies, and your standard Starbucks for our staff time and planning meetings. At times, there is small inconvenience in finding a spot, but the city is full of public domains where you can get together.

4. **When renting for gatherings, we'd recommend you try to stay around 10-20% of your monthly budget.** Since our operating budget has been around $12,000-$15,000 a month, we've never spent over $2000 for monthly space. And on one six-month season where we couldn't find a space within

our budget, we had people remain in their communities and we met in parks once a month for free.

5. **Share space.** In Adullam, we rent our Sunday gathering spot at Denver Seminary. It costs us about $2000 a month and we get essentially 20,000 square feet. Other churches also rent the space during other slots of the week. When we do leadership training, we use a more central gathering space at another church at the cost of $100 a night. I use pubs for our evangelistic "Story of God" trainings, and we rent the Comedy Works Club for our larger parties and all church functions. In the summer, we head to parks once a month to save even more and break up the monotony of inside gatherings.

Time is mammon

Equipping isn't easy, and that's why I'm fine with getting paid to do it. But we still have to do it wisely. Here's some ways to cut time and still do a good job.

Sermon/Teaching Prep

I was taught in seminary that I was unworthy to stand behind the pulpit unless I studied the scripture in the Greek for at least forty hours a week! I remember hearing that and raising my hand, saying, "Excuse me, doctor, I work as a house painter about thirty to forty hours a week. So if I add another forty hours for sermon prep, it doesn't seem to leave much room for . . . well . . . anything!"

He replied, "Well, son, maybe you're not called to lead a church." Because of my naivety and because I believed him about the importance of the sermon, I did both. On our first church plant, I averaged 100 hours of "work" a week, and my wife didn't like me, my kids thought I was always cranky, and I was withering away into a shell of who I was. But I was championing the cause of "good news"! What a farce!

The reality of adult learning is that the average adult listening to us only retains about five to ten percent of the content we've worked so hard to prepare, and by the time they unload the kids at McDonalds an hour after church, they've pretty much forgotten most of what we said. And yet, week after week, we make mammon of our time, thinking that the sermon is the center of disciple-making. But it's not even close! Adults learn primarily through sensory experience, not cognitive downloads, and the acceptance of this fact should unhinge us from this weekly grind that bears so little fruit.

Look, I'm a Bible guy and believe in the power that lies within every syllable. I also believe that we should handle the word of God correctly and make sure we deliver our teaching with accuracy and skill. But I also believe a sermon should be considered one of the ways we teach, not the only way. Understanding this will not only help you focus your time on other disciplines and experiences that will grow disciples, but it will also allow you to find a better balance for your own life.

I now spend five hours a week meditating and preparing to share a scriptural point with our people, and it is far better than when I spent forty hours on it. Spiritual authority no longer comes through our proficiency. It comes through our lives. People follow people because they respect how we live, not because of what we say. And this change in the culture's expectations gives us a new opportunity to be real people with a simple message. I'm not saying all this to cheapen teaching prep. The scriptures are clear that we should take it seriously and do the best job we can. But with all the tools and helps around us, you can significantly cut the prep time down. I used to spend hours reading other ancient saints' stories and applications, cross-referencing a study Bible, and doing word searches. Now, I simply read and meditate on the passage throughout the week, Google the text and read a few commentaries online to make sure I'm not missing a key point of theological clarity, meditate some more, and deliver. I no longer work on three points since adults cannot remember more than one.

As a staff team of bi-vocational leaders, we only give ourselves fifteen minutes a week to plan the Sunday worship gathering. Those who lead our musical worship do not have a practice night since I don't want them to spend valuable time they could be spending with lost friends or their family. I want our people giving their best time to the things that truly bear kingdom fruit, and most of the fruit-bearing activities are not related to the Sunday gathering.

Meetings/Committees

First, try to not to have any. I'm serious. A ton of time is wasted simply because we create committees, and committees have to meet. So limit this time by never having committees. Distribute your workload to your communities. Have each missional community take turns with kids ministry, set up, tear down, benevolence distribution, or anything else you really want done. If you distribute out, you won't have to make up a reason to take up their valuable time or yours.

Yes, you will need a few leadership meetings for those who are holding the ship together and who help facilitate the gathering, but it doesn't have to happen more than once a week. We do gather every Tuesday for two hours with our team of bi-vocational and volunteer leaders. We spend most of the time encouraging each other and talking about needs we see that fall between the crack of the missional communities, but we do give fifteen minutes to planning the church gathering. It's mostly just making sure each element is covered, but that's all that is needed.

In summary, we do value both our gathered essence and our scattered essence. We love to be apart, living missionally and getting most of the work of ministry done as real people during the week. And we love to see each other every week for a church gathering. But we put our best time and money into our scattered, decentralized communities, and it keeps our church gathering rich with relationships, stories, and celebration while costing us very little in time or money. Best of all, both our time and money go to the most important thing. Reaching the least and the lost. Let's now take a look at this.

Cheap conversions

Okay, this is a crass question. What do you think is an appropriate cost per conversion? Can you put a price on such a thing? Consider these true stories.

A church in central Detroit, which used to be one of the most successful churches in the country, began to lose its pull as the city grew around it. Initially it drew some of Detroit's larger donors, positioned as it was in the suburbs. As the city grew, the city and its natural needs grew too close and eventually the money and over half of the church left for safer pastures. In a last ditch effort to survive, the leadership decided to sell their building to a prep school and reposition out where the hottest suburban sprawl was. They got $3 million for their church and then put that down on a $16 million state of the art building. As soon as they opened they packed the 1500 seat sanctuary. Yes, a majority of their growth was transfer growth, but they do have good stories of new conversions. On average, they've seen 100 adults per year come to faith. They saved the church, and even today, it is considered a success story in the city. But is it? The monthly mortgage is $80,000 a month. And the total budget for their 30 staff and building is around $8 million a year. Is that success? The CPC (cost per conversion) is the same as their mortgage.

Each conversion costs them $80,000.

This isn't that expensive according to national averages. One mega church in Denver asked my partner Matt and me to be in on a meeting where they were deciding whether or not to add on to their building. We were helping them move from a program-attractional ministry to one based on incarnational communities. It was going well, but one staff member asked, "Can't we do both at the same time?" He mentioned that people were leaving because the parking was a hassle and thought that if they built on, they would stem the tide a bit. During the meeting they asked our opinion.

"Well, here's the bottom line," I said. Your present budget is $6 million a year for 3000 people. You have on average five adults come to faith a year, so your CPC is about $1.2 million. The expansion you're considering will cost another $12 million and seat another 1200 so that would account for another three to four people, but it would push your CPC up to about $2 million per head." The room was quiet. One elder asked us, "So, what is your CPC at Adullam?" Matt and I looked at each other, Matt did a little figuring and then said, "Two bucks."

They didn't do the expansion, but these two stories speak like a tuba solo inside a quiet library that at some point, you've got to look up from your reality and figure out if it lines up with the reality of the kingdom as modeled by Jesus and count-less thousands, even millions, of people who did not spend this much to reach a friend. I don't know where the line is, but I do know there is a line!

I do realize that a church is more than a conversion project. For the money we spend on the building, we are teaching people, caring for children, providing space for the community to use for funerals and weddings (I hope we do this), and many other helpful functions. So it is too simplistic to add up the total cost and come up with a CPC, but I think you get the point. We have to look at the cost vs. the return and make some adjustments. Here are a few that we've seen that should inspire you.

Church A, realizing that their property was worth $12 million, decided to sell and rebuild for the cost of $2 million to fit its aging and declining congregation. They pocketed $10 million in cash, put $6 million into church planting, $2 million in the bank, and gave the rest to local benevolent non-profits, most of which were not Christian. They lightened their load, increased their legacy, and deepened and improved their street cred within the lost community. Great play!

Church B, realizing that they did not need 40

paid staff to manage 1200 people, shrunk their staff down to 10, keeping only those who could equip the congregation to do the work of ministry, took 50% of the money they saved and sent out two of the laid-off staff to plant another church. They did take a hit as some in the congregation got angry that staff were being laid off, but in two years had grown past their original mark and continue to grow both in number and depth of discipleship as a result. Great play!

Although these are not bi-vocational models such as our own, they still show the benefit of leaning out and lightening up so that the cost of reaching people lines up more with biblical precedent.

Questions that could change your life

1. As we've brought up quite a few ways to lighten the financial load of growing a kingdom community, which adjustments were the most inspiring to you? Which ones freak you out a little?

2. Since time is as valuable a commodity as money, what are some ideas you got about re-allocating your time to things that really make a difference?

3. What should you stop doing right now?

What should you try to give away to others?
What should you start giving your best time
to?

Learning the Labyrinth of Bi-Vocational Life

As we said in the beginning, every Christ follower must accept two God-given vocations or callings. One is your calling to provide and work, and one is your calling to serve Jesus as he extends his kingdom to the world. Those are non-negotiables and are the two greatest privileges we have. We've spent quite a bit of time addressing how this might look as missionary saints re-form church and mission, but what about the reality underneath it all? What about our actual lives? At the end of the day, the church is the people of God, and as such, we are the vessels by which the gospel gets transferred into other lives. You are actually the commodity. Colossians 1:27 says, "To them God has chosen to make known among the Gentiles the glorious riches of this mystery, which is *Christ in you, the hope of glory.*" Did you notice the nuance there? We always say that Christ, by himself, is what changes the world, but here Paul says that it is "Christ in us" that is really the hope of the world. We are the carriers of Christ. That means a truly BiVo life is based on the foundation of how much Christ lives in us. Don't miss this. When I share my story, people too quickly jump to the how-tos of managing business and ministry. But the fact of the matter is that your life is what Jesus will build on and leverage.

The six knacks

My wife is a real estate agent, and many of her clients are young couples in our church. She obviously loves to buy and sell houses for people, and I love it when she makes a little deposit into the Halter family checking account. But even more, Cheryl loves to guide glassy-eyed couples through the preparation of buying a house. Many times, she assesses their reality and finds that they aren't quite ready to make this jump. Sometimes they need to work on their credit score, sometimes they need to put more cash away, and often they need to work through marriage and spiritual issues related to materialism, differing values, and so on. What makes her great, though, is that all of her clients say that she is realistic and encourages them toward their desired goals. The same is true for moving into a healthy BiVo life. We all need to get there, but you need some time to assess where you're at and what you need to work on to get there.

As I have talked with hundreds of successful BiVo's, I've discovered that there are six primary "knacks" that you have to take seriously before you'll truly enjoy the BiVo life. I chose the term "knack" because it communicates growing aptitude, not perfection or having attained something. It's simply that you are developing the knack for something. Here they are in short terms, but toward the end we'll give you a simple pathway to assess yourself on all the knacks and begin a pathway.

Personal Knack

The ability to own one's own life. This category judges personal ownership, motivation, discipline, physical health, optimism, fortitude, work ethic, the ability to multi-task, discipline to plan and schedule time. Essentially one's personal knack is the ability to manage and move yourself.

Family Knack

This assesses for spousal buy in, spousel cohesion, strength of marriage, and the emotional depth of parent to child relationship. Essentially the family knack is the strength and stability of your family to move into mission together.

Relational Knack

Assess for incarnational aptitude, street cred with people, likability, the ability to draw people, woo, energy for humans, network capacity in community, and ability to lead community. Essentially this knack is about whether or not people will want to follow you and be with you and whether or not you will be able to give this level of relational time to people.

Spiritual Knack

This assesses your spiritual stability. Whether you are clear on identity in Christ, your level of pride and humility, your ability to hear and follow God's voice, and your ability to walk by faith. Essentially the spiritual knack is about truly walking with God and letting him lead on an hourly-daily basis.

Financial Knack

This assesses for level of desperation versus stability with money, self-control, living by budget, generosity, ability to handle stress together as a couple. This also assesses for what you have to work with or what God has given you to steward. Your actual cash reality and potential, as well as your assets that can be used for kingdom purposes, house, yard, business office space, other stuff, etc. Essentially this knack is about how well positioned you are to live BiVo.

Skill/Gift Knack

This assesses for clarity and creativeness on your specific skills, gifts, and spiritual gifts that God can use. It includes your network position in the neighborhood or business, how you lead best, as well as your personality style. Essentially this knack is about how God will use you in the world.

Start by taking this quick but powerful assessment. After you get the results, we can also help you evaluate the findings and move toward growth in all knacks. As you grow, the BiVo life will start to come into view. To access the BiVo assessment, go to www.bivonetwork.com.

Leadership Vertigo

Now let's get some practical advice on how to let God leverage your life whether you are fully paid, paid a little, or not paid at all. I always like to say that there's no such thing as a balanced life, but there is a balancing act in learning how the secular and sacred work together.

Life—disaster, celebration, opportunities, God-moments, downtime, Sabbath, mundane, nine-to-five, momentum events, a week in the hospital, planned intentions, and interruptions never work out in a planned way. As I'm writing this, I'm sitting on the tarmac at the St. Louis airport and am now delayed five hours simply because United couldn't find a flight attendant. Most of life isn't actually in our control and days like this will happen all the time. Even though I make a big deal about weekly planning, I've also come to realize you have to hold those plans loosely while holding tightly to divine opportunities. In other words, normal life is generally out of control, but divine living is always available in every moment, so you can control or at least yield to that.

If you are a full time ministerial staff, you have a paycheck, but you also have a natural disequilibrium by being stuck inside a confined job description, building, and the natural expectation that others will have of you if you take the paycheck. If you're a paid staff person at any level of any church, you are essentially on call for whatever happens in the life of your congregation, and most times, when you get the call, it's not good news and you have to adjust your entire world to make that momentary need the priority. Bi-vocational or part-timers will have disequilibrium from having to turn off and on ministry focus at strange times and in intervals that naturally disrupt family flow, work flow, and life flow. And unpaid saints also have a dizzy vertigo in trying to wedge in sacred moments amidst what is otherwise a normal life. All three carry a natural tension, all three require wisdom and the guidance of the Spirit, and all three will cost you something. It's not that important which one you chose, but it is important that you're realistic with the choice you make.

Here are a few points of wisdom.

Two things, not three. I find that every person can do one thing well, stable leaders can do two things well, and only a very rare bird can juggle three things and do them well. In other words, bi-vocational is workable, but tri-vocational is most likely going to be a train wreck. Multi-tasking is an acquired skill, and it's been proven that the more you multi-task, the less functional each task is. So in this life, you have to be realistic about your abilities. I was a house painter, a church planter, a seminary student, and father of a son who had seizures every few hours. I made it about ten years, but that was it. Meltdown!

If you are considering juggling ministry leadership with a normal job, I recommend you only do those two. Don't add anything else. Incarnational ministry has a heavy relational cost, so in order to have space and relational bandwidth, you should try to protect the two spheres as much as you can. Saying NO is a skill you must learn if you are to survive!

This is a good time to remind you again that bi-vocational shouldn't be your end goal. It is a means to get to another desired end goal, and that should be about living as large and as free a life as you can. Here are a few reasons you might want to chose the bi-vocational option.

If you want to try your hand at a "new wineskin" or approach that hasn't been tried or proven before. Entrepreneurs love to try wild, crazy ideas, and some of life's greatest stories come from men and woman willing to think and live outside the box. But you should never expect someone to pay your bills to do it. Denominations won't take the risk, churches won't get behind them, and it will be pretty difficult to get private investors or even your spouse to give it a go. So if you want to live outside the box, be ready to fund it by yourself, at least until it begins to work. Early adopters will always be open to investing in things that show fruit. I think this is why the Apostle Paul, in 1 Thessalonians 2:9 chose to work among people to avoid being a burden to the people to whom he was teaching the gospel. Paul teaches us an important lesson about starting new things. Whether it be a church plant, or fringe missionary or business venture, leaders understand that "speculative ventures" need to be gone after without expecting fast or future financial returns. You need to be able to work without strings attached.

If you want to begin a work that the unchurched culture will respect. Joey Turner, a church planter in Ft. Worth, started a small congregation and also a pub. He knew the church would be something that would grow slowly, and thus he got investors to help build a sweet community pub right in the middle of old Ft. Worth. It was and is a huge hit with the locals, and the business blesses many non-profits, providing space for meetings that local churches never would, as well as giving his church community a natural place to connect without all the religious baggage. See Joey's Story in the appendix.

If you feel called to help pastor a smaller, more rural, or inner city congregation where the people are the point of the mission instead of

the recourses of the mission. Bottom line, many contexts God sends us to will never be able to fully fund even a single pastor, but if these types of people and contexts are on your heart, then you can be like Paul who chose to work among the people so that he would not burden the community (Acts 18:3, 2 Thessalonians 3:7-9).

If your vision for business and mission is so big that you can use your business to fund many ministries and ministers. The great news is that many business owners are successful, and it would be a waste for the kingdom if they left what they were good at and entered church work. If you've got the swag to make big cash, keep going and link your gift with others who can take on other ministry roles.

If in your season of life, you must now care for extended family or aging parents, put children through college, or reposition and downsize. Taking a season to focus on stabilizing your funds can go a long way toward keeping you in the ministry stream for the long haul. Ecclesiastes and the nightly news teach that there are times things work and times they don't.

Seasons are a key part of how God created us to navigate life, and here are a few: Single, newly married, newly married with young kids, married with elementary to high school kids, empty nest, retired. The ones that are most troublesome for BiVo's are the middle three, so be more careful there. A lot more is at stake! If you can, try not to move children during the middle school and high school season unless they lead the charge. The cost can be too high if they are not good at change. Try to ask the question, *Will the decision I'm about to make be good news for my spouse and children?* You don't want your children being the back end or the brunt of a poorly thought out dream. You want to hear God's revealed vision, and I believe in most cases God wants your family to experience good news.

If you're setting yourself up for a life of simple, free ministry. A young man named Tim has become a key figure in our Adullam story. He is gifted, called, and has great natural leadership and commitment to ministry. We brought him in from Baltimore and quickly put him on part-time paid staff overseeing our church gatherings. Everything was going great! Then over a coffee, he said, "Hugh, just a thought, but I'm making a ton of money with my mortgage business and I don't really need the $2000 stipend you're paying me. I do know Kevin could really use it and we need him on the team too, so can I keep doing my ministry job, but do it for free?" Imagine the beauty and freedom that Tim not only gets to live, but the blessing his life is in our network. Tim wins, Kevin wins, and Adullam wins, so I win.

In my case, I chose to stay bi-vocational because I simply enjoy living two lives. I love having a larger band of friends to work along with. I love doing only what I'm good at and letting others do what they are good at. I love doing something different every day and I get energy from multi-tasking and multi-living. But I've also learned that others don't enjoy what I do, so I would persuade you away from bi-vocational life if you can't identify with at least one of these reasons to try it.

I hope these reasons for being bi-vocational give you both vision and reason for taking on two lives.

Suggestion: If you're not sure whether you are cut out for dual life, consider that gifting and personality really matter. That goes not just for you, but also your spouse. You may be cut out for it, but your spouse may not be able to handle it. Assess yourselves together. Again, I highly encourage you to take this specific BiVo assessment we've set up for you. It won't make your decision foolproof, but it will help you get at the actual conversations you need to have with yourself and your spouse.

Practical suggestions to make the bi-vocational life work

I've been trying to coin a new term for bi-vocational because the term seems to communicate that you're choosing to live two lives poorly. But if you're going to try this, you shouldn't do it unless you actually plan to live both lives well. So if you've chosen to manage two lives, here's my best advice for how to thrive in both spheres.

Crazy intentional about organization. It is true with anything. The more you're juggling, the more organized and intentional you'll have to be. If you don't get on the offensive, you'll be on the defensive. And being defensive makes living the good news of Jesus Christ lousy news to your wife, kids, and friends. I have had to develop a commitment to take every Sunday evening to plan out the next week. I sit down, light a candle, pour a Merlot, get my family calendar, and then prayerfully think my way through the next seven days. I would say that if you're not willing to do this first step, you're should not chose bi-vocational life!

Here's how I would suggest you organize your week (this is based on the illustration where you fill the jar with big rocks first, then medium sized rocks, then let God fill in all the cracks and crevices).

Big rocks: have-tos/get-tos

Sabbath: The more I learn about the orientation of Jesus to the Father, the more I've come to realize that God wants us to prioritize an abiding life with him first and then let our work flow from that. Most of us work frantically trying to juggle life, hoping that God will lead us and bless us, but the truth of scripture and the teaching of the Sabbath is that God blesses and favors those who make sure they rest and abide first and then let God build influence from their work. Your physical well being, mental stability, and overall soul care are the deep wells of good news you give to people, so it makes sense that you prioritize this side of life. I am by no means rock solid on this, but I have changed my mindset from guilt to permission-giving when it comes to taking care of myself and the inner life of my family. I consider my physical and mental health as part of my job and calling, so when I work out, take Harley rides, sit with Cheryl on our deck, golf dates, date nights, coffee times, kids' sports, school events, family meals or just a good ol' fashioned nap, I believe I'm prioritizing my Sabbath life. It's a big deal now.

Family time: Even though your Sabbath time may include this, make sure that you also schedule in all the family time, like time watching their athletic and extracurricular school activities, games, plays, etc. Also schedule in family nights or dates with your wife and kids.

Vocation: For me, I give about thirty hours a week to Missio and twenty hours to Adullam. For twenty years, it was house painting, so I obviously have to schedule in the must-dos and the have-tos to be faithful to my commitments to these ministry and provisional callings.

Medium rocks: Should-dos

Leader time: If you get paid from ministry, you must always assess whether you are giving most of your time to equipping others instead of doing ministry for others. As an "equipper," I now give my best time to my best leaders. For me, it is scheduling time with community leaders I coach or new leaders who are trying to start communities. If they do well, our entire movement does better than if I spend my time with nebulous appointments.

Sojourner time: As my gifting is evangelistic, my next commitments are to be with people who do not know Christ. I book coffee times, pub times, work out times together, and whatever I can do to prioritize relationships God is leading me into.

Little rocks: God-gets-tos

Space: I've learned that blocking off "space" or undesignated time is critical for spontaneous ministry to happen. If I block off all day Friday, Wednesday night, and several two to four hour blocks, I tend to fill it with important invites that God brings up. If someone needs a hand, if someone needs to talk, or if I need to do something, I now have space for God to fill it.

Church stuff: The last thing I put in is the activities I must do to help the whole movement. That could be five hours for sermon prep, two hour staff time, a quarterly training I might be doing, etc. You'll find that the things other leaders get paid $90,000 to do for a church can be done on your spare time. I only spend fifteen minutes a week planning our Sunday church gatherings and we've never had a bad Gathering. We prefer that our worship people don't spend a night practicing so that they also get to maximize their own lives. Our staff meet for two hours each week, but about an hour of that is just being together. Funny thing, it all works out just fine.

Caveat: As you learn how to intentionalize the best things, the right things, and the most important things, you'll find there's not much left for nebulous "YES" answers. I used to hem and haw, and then cave to people and their expectations for my time, but I don't anymore. If they ask for a coffee time, I respond, "I'd love to, but can you let me know what you'd like to talk about so that I can decide if I am the best person?" This gives me a chance to shift their need to another person who fits the bill better. As you train yourself, you will also be training your people to be more intentional with their time.

Smart jobs, not just a job

"Smart jobs" are either a job that makes you a lot of money fast *or* a job that helps you connect with people and create social momentum. A super smart job does both. A dumb job, therefore, would be one that does neither. For instance, Lou decided to sell medical equipment. The pay was high and he put himself on a strict financial regimen so that he could remove almost all debt over a five-year span, creating space for a lateral move to run his own insurance agency. This new role gave Lou much more flexibility, and he's now positioned financially for a good forty years of ministry leadership. Tim runs his own mortgage-banking firm which gives him total freedom of his time and he makes enough to live well. My job allows me a lot of time in hotels and on airplanes, so I can keep good communication going with ministry needs back home. Then, when I'm in town, my time is focused. Matt was eighty percent funded through personal support, so he got a two day a week teaching job at a private school and can still give forty hours to ministry. Curt and his wife run a successful house staging company and Curt can handle the administrative duties for this company for fifteen to twenty hours a week. He serves Adullam at about thirty hours a week as a volunteer.

Dumb jobs are those that exhaust you physically, don't make enough money to remove your stress, or have no ability to connect you to people. If that's what you're left with, or you have no idea what you could do to make ends meet, I'd suggest you simply work in the world or work in the church. As the church fades, you'll have to face the music too, so I always encourage everyone to find a trade that can create options. But the reality is that many of us who grew up preparing for full time ministry simply are caught out of position now. Be realistic with where you are and get some counsel before you set your new future in motion.

Don't jump into fantasy land

I'd like to also blow a trumpet in the ear of the purists out there. The ones that have had a growing discontent with your role inside the church and who are about to quit so you can go make the perfect life. BLOWWWWW. That's the trumpet sound. Don't jump out until you have something better to go to. I know you're frustrated and you can't stand some of the duties and meaningless expectations that go on inside the box, but realize that you do have a lot more freedom than you think. I've seen so many leaders, mostly young ones, deconstruct the mother ship and jump out only to find themselves working at Starbucks or Home Depot for ten years without any more time or energy for ministry. I'm not dissuading you from making a courageous lateral or even downward move, but don't go be a pie in the sky dreamer. It ain't any easier out there. So what do you do if you're dying on the inside of a church job? Try to outsmart it. In most cases, without anyone knowing and without downgrading the honest effort you're giving to the measurements of your job description, you can give the same intentionality to your week and still find a ton of space for real people and real ministry. Try that first and if you simply can't live out your calling, then consider the move out.

Bi-vocational is not the goal, it's a means to a goal

Remember, being bi-vocational isn't the goal and it's not necessarily any better or worse than being fully paid from ministry or fully paid from the world. The goal is to live as healthy a kingdom life as you can, being faithful to obey God and free up as much time for people as you can. There are a thousand scenarios that can make the kingdom of God tangible for you and the friends you want to reach. You just have to find out what it might look like for you and move toward your preferable future. But don't wait until you have it all figured out. Start making small choices this week and literally start doing what you want to do later now. In time, you should be able to keep increasing your influence and impact. To get at that, ask these questions:

1. If money were not an issue, what would I truly spend my time doing? If money is no longer an issue, how can you start giving significant time to ministry functions now? Who can you serve? Who can you team up with?

2. Since money is an issue, where should I start leaning out my life, expenses, and activities so that I can get to my preferred future?

3. Could I move toward this preferred future if I left or adjusted my present employment to take steps toward another way of funding my livelihood (that could be leaving a pastoral job or secular job)?

4. If you're being paid from ministry, how can you adjust to be more of an equipper to those who are doing the ministry instead of being a chaplain for Christians who are not doing the work of ministry?

5. What types of skills, business ventures, or volunteer opportunities could you move toward that have a direct kingdom influence on the culture? Should you start one, or find one that already exists?

Questions that could change your life

1. Your life is the commodity God uses to change the world. With knowing that, what aspect of your home life or personal life might need some work? Where do you feel God helping you become deeper?

2. Are you a vigilant planner? If not, what weekly rhythms will you begin so that you can learn to live multiple callings? Be specific. What do you need to get organized?

3. Create your own jar of rocks. What are the big, medium, and small rocks?

Epic Failure

A few months ago, I was asked to speak at a very unique conference. It was called the Epic Failure conference. Unlike so many conferences that tout the twenty-five fastest growing churches and applaud the more dynamic communicators, or at least those who would clearly fit the "winner" category, this conference was for those who have tasted bitter defeat in ministry, church, and personal life.

To encourage the downtrodden, I went to the passage in Hebrews where it talks about being surrounded by a great cloud of witnesses. This passage is usually brought up to inspire people to live hugely successful lives, but in reality it's about living a life in view of so many who have worked hard for God without seeing much result.

The scriptures are pretty clear about who the heroes were and are. They are those who have sacrificed for the Gospel, who have stood faithful in view of physical death, and who have given up everything for their love of the king and his kingdom. As I imagine the day when I will get to meet them in heaven, I think it might actually be awkward to jump in the middle of their support group and share all the successes I had. Can you imagine the looks on the face of Moses, Rahab, David, Sampson, and so many others who made grave errors that cost them a ton, who were sliced in two by swords, burned to death in front of their families, or ripped apart by lions in an outdoor amphitheater! I guarantee that you're going to feel much better when you sit down next to them and share the stories you are now presently lamenting. In other words, your proudest moments will be the stories where it didn't work out, where it didn't go well, when it cost you everything, or when you stayed with that miserable ministry post over the long haul. You are going to want these stories when you get to heaven, even though they don't feel really good down here.

I've come to realize that I have made the right decisions only half the time in my life. I bat fifty percent when it comes to hearing from God correctly and faithfully executing the plan. The other fifty percent are lousy decisions and short-sighted plans, and I've got a stack a mile long of goofy dreams gone bad and wasted meetings with people I should have never met with. Whereas batting fifty percent is great if you play baseball, it's a terrible reality for what our lives actually amount to. It literally means I've wasted half of my life! Dangit!

But here's the great news. God loves people who take healthy swings at the plate and who also strike out. You and I will never get in trouble for visions gone awry or exploits unrealized, so don't lament your epic failures, but do learn from them.

Cool scars

Although the scars of failure we received in the battle of kingdom living are badges of honor, our goal shouldn't be to try to fail. Duh! Some of the scars come legitimately from doing the right things for the right reason, but if you're like me, some of the scars come as self-inflicted wounds, and those we should try to minimize.

I remember pulling into my driveway with the top of my jeep off and watching my two high school girls gasp as I dragged my bloody body out of the car. "Dad, why are you bleeding everywhere?" I sheepishly replied, "I went mountain biking without my shirt or helmet and had a bit of a spill down a rocky embankment." Those scars are still on my back and I only have myself to blame!

Flack from the enemy is cool, but friendly fire or shooting ourselves in the foot or the face should be avoided at all costs. So if you feel that to date you've been an epic failure, stop sucking your thumb and using the miseries of ministry as an excuse or justification to pull off the front lines. Be courageous enough to look in the mirror and into the face of God and commit the next season of your life to a new story and a new opportunity. He still has "good works that he's prepared for you to do." Some of the failures don't have to repeat themselves if you consider breaking out of old paradigms. You do have options.

More options now available

As I've pointed out in this entire book, many of the failures we've experienced both personally and in ministry have come from a very unnatural environment we call consumer church. It costs too much and therefore puts incredible pressure on us to prop up the system to keep our livelihood going. It's made heroes only of those who could speak eloquently or lead a large multitude into a shallow pool, but we've died in the process. As we got sucked into the vortex of putting on the Sunday performance for a group of people that may or may not want to actually follow Jesus, we shot arrows into our own souls and stopped following him ourselves. Everything we did was under the guise of the language of discipleship, but in the end we can barely recall actual moments of being a disciple ourselves. We weren't designed to do everything for everyone. We weren't designed to tie ministry to money. We weren't designed to go it alone. And we weren't designed to keep everyone happy. Jesus loved the multitude. He fed them on occasion, healed them and taught them, but he didn't give his best time or even the majority of his time to attenders or church shoppers. He gave his best effort to those who would someday give their lives for the kingdom of God. We were called to be disciples and to make disciples. That is all. And that will be more meaningful.

Good news is good news

We can't be people who share the good news if the gospel remains crappy news for us personally. I always tell people and leaders that if our church ever became too churchy or lost the joy of being a family of friends and fellow missionaries, I'd just shut it down. But I would not change how I live. At some point we all have to decide how we want to follow Jesus and stick to it. My first church almost cost me my marriage, my financial stability, my sanity, and my joy. This last one has given all that back. The kingdom of God really is good news if you don't let yourself be sucked back into the old forms. It's not good news to have your spouse always anxious over money. It's not good news that your kids never get to do anything fun or go on a vacation because dad is too busy or too broke from serving everyone else. You were meant to lead, but that doesn't mean you have to lead the way you used to. People will still come to you for things, but they don't have to suck you dry or come to you for things they can get somewhere else or provide for themselves. You don't have to do ministry in a silo, trying to keep people liking you. You can actually be yourself and live out the unique passions God has put on your heart. And you can do that with friends who want the same thing you do.

As we've said, the world will continue to change and most likely the church under its present business model and discipleship model will collapse, or at least be altered beyond recognition. The ones who get ahead of the curve now or skate to where the puck is going will be the best positioned to not only survive through the tremors, but also thrive!

Find a job you enjoy and work it with joy. Find some friends and divvy up the work. This is where the kingdom always leads, so get back in the game, get ahead, and enjoy some good news yourself.

Questions that could change your life

1. What are your epic failures? What has been formed in you through these apparent failures?

2. Picture yourself in Heaven sitting around with all the other epic losers. What scars will you be most proud of sharing with the group?

3. Take a moment and thank God for the costs and the pain you've been able to share on His behalf. Consider re-upping and give God permission to use your life again.

Cheap Legacy

Don't ride the pine on the bema seat

As we close up shop on this discussion, let me remind you of a biblical truth that should be the plumbline for all your decisions. In Romans 14:10 and 2 Corinthians 5:9, the scriptures reference a moment of judgement we all will face before God. A bema seat is mentioned which is a raised bench where a judge sits, or in this case, where we will go toe-to-toe and eye-to-eye with Christ. The scriptures say that we might be told, "Well done, my good and faithful servant," which also suggests that Jesus can also give us the thumbs down for how we had lived life and managed the tasks he had ordained for us to do.

I've often thought about this moment and I've decided I don't care if Jesus says, "Halter, you were awesome, the best one I've ever seen." I'd settle for, "Halter, you were a blast to watch!" I'm not looking for an A-rating, but I certainly don't want to have him say, "Hugh . . . I modeled true leadership, I gave you clear instructions to make disciples or apprentices of my kingdom, but instead you wasted your time managing church services, consumer Christians, and worrying about all sorts of things I never asked you to do. I don't care that you grew the church from 100 to 500, I don't care that you wrote books that people thought were cute, and I'm not impressed that you got your twitter followers up to 5000. All I asked you to do was make people who looked, smelled, and acted like I did."

The bema seat doesn't have to be a judgment seat. It can be an incredible moment where you and I will get to see Jesus smile and say, "Thanks for caring about what I cared about and for sacrificing your reputation, your finances, and your personal security for the sake of my kingdom." I want to hear that and even more see the face of Jesus warm up to how I lived my life, more than anything in the world.

Repositioning yourself

I'm assuming that as you read this book, most of you, like me, will feel a bit foolish about where we have spent our time and how we have viewed our calling. About now you may be thinking, "I'm going to really change my ways from here on out." For some of you who are young, you can get going now and avoid the pitfalls and wasted time that many of us older folks have.

But for many others, I realize that there is great pain in trying to reposition. You have worked in the church, or around the Temple, your whole life. You were never asked to develop other skills other than the God stuff, and now you're forty-five, fifty-five, sixty-five, or even older and it is brutal to think about how to get back to the street level Jesus life. You may be asking, *How will I pay the bills? How do I start a new career at this age? Do I have any real skills anyone in the world is looking for? I have no retirement, no pension, and no clue!*

If any of these thoughts are yours, I do feel incredible weight for you. You are in the toughest spot as the church transitions. I can't make up any easy answers for you as I don't have any, but here are a few "repositions" that I've seen and heard about that may help you think outside the box. Every one of these pastors has made significant changes in his fifties and sixties.

Joe resigned from his church just before it was about to shut down, downsized everything by selling his home, toys, and even his time-share vacation rental. He and his wife moved into a low-income trailer park that had 300 families, became the "host family" that provided free rent, and had incredible impact as the "chaplain" to many hurting people. They lived off of $1800 a month, but Joe for the first time in forty years of ministry saw God use him evangelistically. He emailed me and said, "I've never had more fun and felt more alive than I do now."

Gary left a missions agency after his personal support slowly dwindled. Seeing the writing on the wall, he began to transition into a role at a small Christian college, teaching missions and church planting. His salary was cut in half, but he's making it and feels very thankful that he has repositioned to working with young leaders.

Hank used to be the teaching pastor at a mega-church. Unable to justify his salary and how empty he felt spiritually, he resigned at the age of fifty-two and went into partnership with a consulting agency, creating videos that teach employees key skills. His salary went down by one third, but he is using his speaking gifts to serve the world.

Larry (my favorite story) is seventy-one. He was a man who said, "I have no skills except for loving people . . . and they don't pay much for that!" I prayed with him over the phone and then got this email a few months later:

> Hugh . . . I am now one of the greeters at my local Walmart. I get paid minimum wage and all I do all day long is shake hands and get shopping carts for customers. I love it! I seem to be able to average one signifi-cant conversation a day where people tell me about their whole life and some of the best ministry I've ever done is now happening. I am draining my retirement, but I don't care. I'm so happy to wake up every day!

These stories have been a light to so many, and I hope you are realizing the vast opportunity your life can still have. As I always say, "If you ain't dead, God ain't done using you."

A good death
Nothing is meant to last forever, and if you've done a good job keeping things lean and nimble, you will be able to make strategic lateral, down-ward, or upward moves without the constraints that

keep people trying to just stay alive. Jesus taught that things have to die in order to give life to new things.

Remember, God is building his church. And when we view the church as he does, that is as a network of worldwide disciples, we can let go of buildings, church names, and relational networks with more trust in what God is doing. I'm not bringing this up so that you have more ammo to pull out of something that is hard or that you aren't enjoying. For sure, every season of ministry comes with weeks and years we wish we could get out of. But I am saying this because very few of us are built or called to stay at the same place with the same people for sixty years. Most of us will change our area of missional focus four to ten times over our lives, and a nimble set up will allow you to follow God quicker and more faithfully.

Leaving well is the key to a full legacy. So many leaders and their churches hang on for dear life to the bitter, ugly end while others with joy in their hearts rally the remnant and start praying about how to hand off or hand down the assets of the kingdom they are still entrusted with. I've seen pastors get out of the way and take early retirement from the church to let the next leadership wave curl quicker. I've seen twenty elderly saints pray on their feeble knees for younger church planters to give their building to, or elder boards downsizing huge asset rich buildings to give a large majority of the money away to new works. There is a good way to die and a bad way to die, and the call of the kingdom is to look for the best types of death.

Questions that could change your life

1. Regardless of your age, are you preparing to die well? What could be some legacy pieces to the story of dying in your context? What could you pass on to the next generation of leaders?

2. If God were to burn away everything that wasn't about him during your life and ministry, what do you think will remain? What are you truly proud of right now?

Final Words

It is easy to see that God is changing the church right before our eyes. We are caught in a painful transition, but the tension is chock full of new opportunities, not just in regard to ministry vocation, but in learning the art of living well in the kingdom. I hope you are one of the courageous who will stop complaining and drop to your knees, giving God permission to lead you into a new story. Pray for clarity of vision, friends to go on mission with, wisdom to know how to leave, what to start, where to work, how to grow a business, how to leverage your time and resources, and how to love Jesus with everything you have. We are all called to full time work, and at some point we will get to see Jesus and shut it all down. We will never have to struggle with provision, with finding balance between family time and ministry. We'll never have to try to "reach" people anymore and all of our sacrifices will end. We will get to rest forever. Knowing that, take the remaining seconds, days, and years and commit to making the most of your days, filling them with time for people!

I pray God's richest wisdom and joy over you as you serve and live!

—Hugh

Back Stories

BREWED & the BLEND of Sacred and Secular—Joey's Story

I came to faith in Young Life. A woman of normal persuasion entered my life and led me into a community where I found Jesus. The impact of her life not only changed the course of my spiritual condition, it also called me to ministry. I spent fifteen years on staff with Young Life and learned the value of engaging culture in their space as a real person.

Funny thing though. This incarnationally-based approach to living eventually got muddled as I took a job at a really great mega church. I guess it was the natural progression or my weariness of raising missionary support. It didn't take long to realize the distinct difference between the organic, incarnational style of Young Life compared to the often corporate event-driven ministry world I now lived in. Over the years, my time and energy began shifting to help make Sunday mornings a success for all. I began to spend a majority of my time in meetings to plan our church service, including spending hours on announcements and power point slides for the upcoming week. The problem wasn't necessarily our body focusing on Sunday mornings, but rather that my evangelistic gifting and desire to be among the lost was all but removed. I was dying inside and began questioning how to reposition my passion and gifting back toward the streets.

The process of "leaving" the church building took two years. The final straw was reached on a trip I took to China with some friends. I was amazed at how organic believers and church leaders had to be in order to survive, even thrive for that matter. I couldn't believe how many students were interested in what we had to say about Jesus! I finally asked our missionary friend how he was able to create such a following with non-believing Chinese students. What he told me changed my whole outlook on what life outside the church walls would be like back home.

He said, "Joey, I tried for a few years to find a way to engage with these students, and they wouldn't have anything to do with me. But when I started working for the business, instantly they not only engaged with me, but saw me in a new light."

After ten days of absorbing my friend's "Business as Mission" approach, I knew I had gained a key to help me solve the puzzle of how to engage the eighty percent in Ft. Worth when I returned. I knew we would plant a new church, but as I met with would-be missionary friends, our mission became clear. The seeds were planted and our church called The Field took root. Our investment in the city was born.

We spent our first year asking, *How can we add value to our city?* If we could figure out a good way to address this question, the rest would take care of itself. As we listened, a local business became our solution. Our desire was to create a place that would give people a taste of the kingdom. After a long process of listening, a financial plan was put together and a business for mission was created called BREWED, a local coffee house/pub.

BREWED's vision morphed into a full-blown restaurant that serves handcrafted coffee, local craft beer, and locally-sourced entrees. It took us two years to open, and we had several big decisions to make along the way. It was very important for BREWED to not be a "bait and switch" type of operation. In other words, we didn't want The Field (our church plant) to be tied to BREWED, or it would kill the process of gaining an identity with the locals we were trying to serve. If the community confused our mission and thought BREWED was tied to The Field, it would just be another Christian trick to try and get outsiders to come to their church. This was not our intention at all! We wanted to give a gift to our city with no strings attached.

Because of this vision, BREWED become a

for-profit entity and is not connected to The Field in anyway. Our church doesn't even meet at BREWED due to our sensitivity to making sure people don't feel like we are trying to push them to join our "thing." We took one of the ugliest buildings in town and turned it into a beautiful space we all are proud of. We have also hired over fifty employees and tried our best to train, empower, and treat them like they have never been treated before in the industry. We have truly added value to our city.

For a year, our team spent their time finding creative ways to serve our city. Besides spending all our time and money dining locally, we also listened. For instance, we partnered with our local neighborhood association and hosted a pop-up dog park for one day. Our neighborhood loves their pets, but didn't have a dog park anywhere nearby. We wanted to provide a snapshot of what it might be like if we had a dog park. After all, the kingdom is about creativity and producing people that love. We hoped to be the catalyst for someone with the passion to step up and create positive change in our city.

So, on a hot Texas July day, we threw up a fence in our local community park, provided craft beer from a local brewery, and had a few hundred people show up and celebrate with us. On another occasion, we hosted a "hot yoga in the park" event to serve the growing yoga population. Our focus to add value to the city led us to find new ways to support local businesses and to showcase their products and talents in our restaurant. At BREWED, we believe collaboration is the new competition. We believe that the more people we work with rather than compete with, the more it will lead to better business and, of course, better relationships. Because we were so intent on adding value to our city, by the time it was time for BREWED to open, we had created raving fans!

Our vision for BREWED was to become "the locals' living room." And it has.

I will leave you with this, and if you miss everything else, please hear this . . . it's not about a cool, hip new restaurant. It's about leaning into your neighborhood to find ways to add value and serve. Jesus our King stepped into our world to do just that, and we are called to obey his teaching and do the same. Please let me know where your journey takes you!

—Joey Turner

Joey is a true entrepreneur in business and ministry. He is co-owner of BREWED, a unique coffee pub in Fort Worth, Texas and the Lead Catalyst of The Field, a missionally-focused church.

Twitter: @joeyt
Facebook: http://www.facebook.com/joey.turner.9
Instagram: JAVAJOEYFW

BREWED—
www.brewedfw.com
Facebook: BREWED
Twitter: @BREWEDfw

The Field—
www.thefieldfw.org

"Relationships Matter" —Dave's Story

For nine years, I served as a pastor at two great churches in the Denver area. I enjoyed many aspects of my job as a pastor and I felt very fortunate that I was able to make a living doing vocational ministry. But, deep down I knew that I was supposed to be doing something else. I was constantly dreaming about what it would be like to spend my time experimenting with new ways of making the gospel tangible for others. As a result, I knew that I needed to find a different way to provide for my family.

I felt stuck. I had worked in vocational ministry since graduating college and my resume contained references to organizations with names like "The Next Level" and "Warehouse:180." The idea of interviewing and getting hired for a "real job" seemed like a long shot. However, all of that changed as a result of one relationship.

Todd was an elder at my church. He was also a successful business owner with a huge heart for the kingdom. Todd and I became fast friends as a result of our mutual love of sports and Jesus. As our friendship evolved, we talked often about different ways that we might be able to really "move the needle" in our city. One day Todd invited me out to lunch and put a proposal in front of me that seemed too good to be true. He offered to put me on his payroll as a full-time employee. But there was a catch...he didn't want me to work "full-time" for his company. It was a unique job description to say the least. For approximately 20 hours a week, he asked me to do the following for his company:

Community Involvement – help his employees to engage with volunteer opportunities in our community.

Client Relations – build and maintain relationships with some of his key clients.

Employee Care – serve as a "staff chaplain" and oversee team-building activities.

With the rest of my time (twenty to thirty hours a week), Todd encouraged me to pursue my ministry dreams. He didn't ask me for a formal ministry plan or for a list of metrics. He simply told me to keep him in the loop and to pass along stories of how I saw God working. On both a business and ministry level, the results of this arrangement have surpassed our wildest dreams.

When it comes to growing a business, Todd believes that it's all about relationships. This is one of the reasons that he asked me to build and maintain friendships with some of his key clients. Many of the skills that I learned as a pastor have served me well in the world of client relations. Making friends and talking with people about their lives came very naturally for me and I quickly found myself forming deep relationships. This is not the norm in the business world where the majority of work relationships never dip below the surface. Many of Todd's clients went out of their way to tell him how much they enjoyed spending time with me, and talking about things that really matter.

Our efforts to become a business that gives back and cares for employees have also been extremely successful. We established a "serve days" program in which each employee is given two paid days each year to volunteer with a non-profit organization of their choice. We turned our annual company party into a fundraiser and have now given over $210,000 to a homeless shelter here in our community. In a relatively short amount of time, we have become know as a company that cares about people in need.

Since going to work for Todd, my formal "ministry" work has taken on a life of its own. I have spent much of my time helping pastors and churches work together to meet the needs of the poor in our area. Over the last 15 years, I have been a part of a number of great programs and initiatives that have helped people grow closer to God. However, I can honestly say that what I am doing now is the best use of my time and energies when it comes to kingdom impact. As a result of my new work, I have been able to lead a neighboring movement that mobilized over 70 churches and 45k people in the Denver Metro area alone. To learn more about my story, check out the book *The Art of Neighboring*.

The freedom and margin that Todd has built into my job description has made it possible for me to serve as "kingdom bridge builder" in our city. I am learning that the thing that the business world and the vocational ministry world have in common is this - It's all about relationships.

I believe that Todd and I have discovered a powerful and effective model that is reproducible. I have no idea what lies ahead. What I do know is that today I woke up thinking, "I have the best job in the world."

Dave Runyon spends most of his time helping government, business, and faith leaders unite around common causes in the Denver Metro area. He serves as the executive director of CityUnite (www.cityunite.org). Previously, Dave served as a pastor at Foothills Community Church and The Next Level Church. He is the co-author of *The Art of Neighboring*, which was published by Baker Books in 2012 (www.artofneighboring.com). Dave speaks locally and nationally encouraging leaders to work together to serve the common good. He and his wife, Lauren, have four kids and do not plan to have any more.

Welcome to the BiVo Network

As you can tell from this book, our desire is to help you live a BiVo life. You are not alone in this life, or crazy for living this life. All you need is a family to check in with and resources to make the BiVo life easier and cheaper. This is why we are providing the BiVo network. If you register at www.BiVonetwork.com, you'll find a community and resources that you'll keep coming back to. At BiVonetwork.com you'll have access to the BiVo assessment, supercheap books, webinars, training opportunities, stories of other BiVo's, daily prompts to encourage you each day, as well as access to our national Missio team and helpful resources for your life, regardless of whether you are in vocational ministry or secular ministry. www.missio.us.

About Hugh

Hugh Halter is a church planter, pastor, consultant, and missionary to the US. He is the national director of Missio and is the lead architect of Adullam, a congregational network of Missional communities in Denver, Colorado. He is author of *The Tangible Kingdom*, *AND...the gathered & scattered church*, *TK Primer*, *Sacrilege* and *FLESH*. Hugh is an advocate for disoriented God seekers and loves to inspire and re-orient leaders around incarnational mission in any form of church. To find Hugh & other books he's written or to book Hugh for speaking, go to www.hughhalter.com as well as Facebook & @hughhalter on Twitter.

Hi Friends,

As I mentioned throughout the book, the BiVo lifestyle is for everyone. Whether you are in vocational ministry looking to add a business position to your life or you are already in business looking for how to leverage your life for mission we have two helpful resources for you.

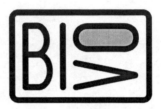

Missio (**www.missio.us**) invites you to join the BiVo network. Through the BiVo network you can access:

- BiVo Assessment: A 20-minute practical assessment that will help you consider possibilities and pitfalls of the BiVo life. The BiVo assessment will give you critical information the "knacks" you need to make the most of BiVo living.

- BiVo subscriptions that will give you access to monthly BiVo webinars on practical issues, BiVo blogs, and access to our BiVo team.

- BiVo learning communities. If you wish to be linked together for year long learning communities to help coach and support BiVo life, business, or mission, consider this more substantive coaching environment.

All BiVo resources listed can be found at **www.missio.us** or **www.bivonetwork.com**.

The other resource we are proud to connect you to is Five Capitals, offered by 3DM.

3DM (**www.weare3dm.com**) has been a longstanding partner with Missio and now BiVo, and their Five Capitals initiative is the very best starting place for marketplace leaders who are asking questions about discipleship and mission in the workplace.

Five Capitals offers content, coaching, consulting, and specialized Learning Communities designed to empower and equip Christian marketplace leaders to live an integrated life of discipleship and mission in their personal and professional lives. Find out about upcoming opportunities at **www.fivecapitals.net**.

BiVo Assessment

Welcome to the BiVo Assessment!

Before you take this assessment, remember that the BiVo life is for everyone in the sense that we all have a calling to live a kingdom life, working with God in his purposes in the world, and we all must work to sustain our lives and that of our family. This test is not a pass/fail but instead will help you discern at what level you can manage these two callings.

Every person must consider 6 key "knacks" for BiVo living.

1) *Personal Knack:* The ability to own & manage one's own life

2) *Family Knack:* The strength, stability, and cohesion of marriage and family dynamics.

3) *Relational Knack:* The capacity to manage relational time as well as your natural 'street cred' with people around you.

4) *Spiritual Knack:* Clarity of spiritual depth, focus, strength and calling.

5) *Financial Knack:* The ability to manage resources and steward what God is giving you and will give you.

6) *Skill/Gift Knack:* What you have under the "hood." Your gifts, talents, aptitudes, leadership style and passions.

To access the BiVo assessment, go to <u>www.bivonetwork.com</u>. After you receive your personalized results return to the BiVo Network to get analysis help and other resources to help you on your way.

Hugh

CPSIA information can be obtained at www.ICGtesting.com
Printed in the USA
BVOW02s0848120314

347380BV00002B/30/P

9 780983 086444